Function justifies an organ, no matter how strange the organ may appear in the eyes of those who are not accustomed to see it functioning.
—Igor Stravinsky, *The Poetics of Music*

The stop motions are as simple as possible without interfering with their effectiveness. The trumpets over the calender rolls are stationary, and act only as condensers. They are adjustable, and may be readily lengthened or shortened to bring the nose nearer or further from the bite of the calender rolls.

The can motion acts upon the filling of the can; and we also can apply a general can motion to act when any number of yards of sliver have been delivered. If desired to detect very light ends coming from the cards we advise the mechanical or "spoon" back stop motion as being adapted to stop the frame when any end passes over them which is materially lighter than the weight to which they have been adjusted. This adjustment is effected by the small weight seen hanging from the spoon. This may be swung out or in to make each spoon more or less sensitive as desired.
—*The Lowell Machine Shop at Lowell, Massachusetts: Carding Machinery* (catalogue and service manual)

1966 also saw the introduction of Tutti, Barbie and Skipper's Little Sister, and her twin brother, Todd. Smaller than Skipper, these little dolls were a delightful addition to the Barbie family. Together, Barbie, Ken, Midge, Allan, Skipper, Skooter, Ricky, Francie, Tutti and Todd all made up the "American Dream Family" and their friends. The couture period, like President Kennedy's life, was over almost before it began.
—A. Glenn Mandeville, *5th Doll Fashion Anthology*

SUBMISSIONS

The editors welcome submissions of fiction, poetry, & literary essays. Send submissions, correspondence, & all other queries to *3rd bed*
17 Union Avenue
Jamaica Plain, MA 02130. Please include a SASE. We also accept electronic submissions & hypertext through our webpage: 3rdbed.com.

SUBSCRIPTIONS

3rd bed is published biannually.
Individuals: $14
Institutions: $16
Outside the US: $16
Individual copies: $8
Make all checks payable to *3rd bed*.

DISTRIBUTION

Small Changes
316 Terry Avenue North
Seattle, WA 07110

Small Press Distribution
154 Christopher Street
Suite 3C,
New York, NY 10014
theliterarymagazinekiosk.com

Bernhard DeBoer
113 E. Centre Street
Nutley, NJ 98109.

EDITOR	Vincent Standley
FICTION EDITOR	M. T. Anderson
POETRY EDITOR	Hermine Meinhard
WEB & ART EDITOR	Paul McRandle
NONFICTION EDITOR	Mary-Kim Arnold
DESIGNER	Dunja Marton
WEB DESIGNER	Kirstin Fenn Chappell
ASSOCIATE POETRY EDITOR	Andrea Baker
ASSOCIATE FICTION EDITOR	Matthew Derby
FOUNDING EDITORS	Christopher Kennedy & James Wagner

3rd bed copyright © 2001
by 3rd Bed, Inc.
ISSN: 1523-6773
ISBN: 0-9709428-1-8

CAROLINE GILMAN	7	Oracles for Youth
ALAN SONDHEIM	20	living in mediaspace 68 (Untitled)
KIM PARKO	24	1.5
ELAINE EQUI	26	Courtesans Lounging After and in Keeping with H. D.
DANIEL BORZUTZKY	28	Bed Time with William James
RUTH DANON	31	Construction Stuck on the Story Hypothetical Little Testament X Marks the Spot
BRYSON NEWHART	42	Widdershins
CYNTHIA CRUZ	53	Wild and Waste Seacliff Manor Are Then Seen and Pursued
RAY GONZALEZ	56	Appearance Appetite The Mind Reader Diego
MARK O'NEIL	61	Origin of Black Flies
PATRICIA EAKINS	67	The Other Side
MICHAEL IVES	83	The Four Fingers of the Left Hand The Skeptic's Anatomical Parable of Sight as an Infinite Regression Kenosis

MARK DeCARTERET	92	ode to antarctica title
MANDEE WRIGHT	94	Juxtaposition
RAPPEL	104	Senoj
PETER MARKUS	109	Girl
KATHRYN RANTALA	111	Sisters
CHAD McCAIL	113	Alien Genital
VIRGIL SUÁREZ	122	A Closer Look at the Details from the St. Peter Altarpiece, St. Peter Martyr by Alonso Berruguete, 1488-1561
ROBYN SCHIFF	124	"Jade Cabinet and One Last Thing," Anonymous Imagination
ROBERT COOVER	127	Lucky Pierre Thaws Out
KEVIN SAMPSELL	137	Flying Horses
CHRISTOPHER KENNEDY	140	Decomposition #249 Trivia The Broken Lock
NORMAN LOCK	143	Opera with Moon Snails The Opera of the Drowned The Opera of Desire
CORMAC JAMES	149	The Disappearance of Miss Effie Skinner
CONTRIBUTORS	168	

ORACLES FOR YOUTH
BY
CAROLINE GILMAN
(1852)

—— DIRECTIONS ——

Let some one hold the book, and ask one of the questions. The answers being all numbered, the girl or boy who is questioned chooses a number, and the person who holds the book reads the answer to which that number belongs, aloud. For instance:

    Question. What is your character?
    Answer. I choose No. 3.

Questioner reads aloud:

    No. 3   Gentle tempered, sweet and kind,
           to no angry word inclined.

WHAT IS YOUR CHARACTER?

THIRTY ANSWERS.

---

1. Very careful, I suppose,
   Since so nice and clean your clothes.

2. Rather careless, I must think,
   Since you often spill your ink.

3. Gentle tempered, sweet and kind,
   To no angry word inclined.

4. Sometimes you in fretful mood
   Rather saucy are, and rude.

5. You your lessons try to know,
   When to school you faithful go.

6. You your lessons sometimes miss;
   What a sad affair is this!

7. When you're summoned from your bed,
   Not a grumbling word is said.

8. When you're eating something nice,
   All around must have a slice.

9   To your parents still, I find,
     You respectful are, and kind.

10 No coarse words you ever say,
     Whether angry or at play.

11 You would never tell a lie,
     Rather would you starve or die.

12 On the holy Sabbath day
     You avoid all idle play.

13 Teachers never can complain
     That your manners give them pain.

14 Never, if in sport or pain,
     Do you take God's name in vain.

15 You esteem it perfect fun,
     When you make or hear a pun.

16 You are fond of serious books;
     I can tell it by your looks.

17 Passionate in temper you;
     But 't is quickly over too.

18 By yourself you like to roam,
     From your playmates and your home.

19 With but one companion sweet,
     You would walk the public street.

20 Social is your mood, and gay;
    You with many love to play.

21 You a foolish trick possess;
    What it is I pray you guess.

22 When a habit bad you take,
    That bad habit you will break.

23 Some one said, you "bite your nails;"—
    But I never tell such tales.

24 Generous and kind your mood,
    Always aiming to do good.

25 What you have begun to do,
    That you firmly will pursue.

26 You a resolution make,
    Which a trifling thing will break.

27 Sometimes cross, and sometimes sad,
    Sometimes kind, and sometimes glad.

28 When you do select a friend,
    That affection knows no end.

29 Very fickle is your love;
    Still from friend to friend you rove.

30 Pious thoughts from you ascend;
    You will make your God your friend.

WHAT ARE YOUR FAVORITE NAMES?

THIRTY-THREE ANSWERS.

---

1. You like Eliza, you like Sue,
   You like Sally, Sarah too.

2. You like Mary and Maria,
   You like Peter and Sophia.

3. You like Thomas and Amelia,
   You like Charley and Cornelia.

4. You like Isaac, so do I,
   You like Julius, you know why.

5. You like David, you like Arthur,
   You like Rosamond and Martha.

6. You like Benjamin and James;—
   'T is hard to think of all these names.

7. You like Joe and Henrietta,
   You like George and Violetta.

8. You like Catherine and Teresa,
   Christiana and Louisa.

9   You like Esther, Margaret,
　　　Emmeline and Harriet.

10   You like Fred and Adeline,
　　　Justina too, and Valentine.

11   You like Nathan and Eugene,
　　　And Archibald to come between.

12   You like Jane and Theodore,
　　　Rosaline and Eleanor.

13   You like Lucy and Pamela,
　　　Or Alonzo and Cecilia.

14   You like Henry's name, in truth,
　　　And Sam becomes an honest youth.

15   You like Virginia and Stephen,
　　　And Mary Anne to make it even.

16   You like Charlotte, you like Ellen,
　　　You like Francis, you like Helen.

17   You like Rebecca more than Ruth,—
　　　The names half puzzle me, in truth.

18   You like Clara and Susannah,
　　　And Alexander too, and Hannah.

19   You like Valeria and Amanda,
　　　And Nathaniel, 't is so handy.

20 Daniel and Robert you approve,
    Emma and Ephraim, too, you love.

21 You like Richard best of all,
    Though sometimes you Octavius call.

22 Caroline is your delight,
    And Julia you love day and night.

23 William and Lydia sound quite sweet,
    Fanny and Abby oft you greet.

24 Laura, Moses, Isabel,
    Edward and John, you like them well.

25 Augustus and Elizabeth
    You love to say with every breath.

26 Eugenia, Alwyn, Maurice, all,
    But Alfred oftenest you call.

27 You love Louis and Floranthe,
    Or dear Agnes or Ianthe.

28 Sweet the name of Adelaide;
    And Clarissa is often said.

29 Joanna's name you sometimes call,
    And Timothy the most of all.

30 Andrew and Edmund you call out,
    And Christopher you often shout.

31   Edwin, and Gilbert following on,
Or Gregory or Jonathan.

32   Humphrey, Lawrence, Jacob too,
And next to Louis you like Hugh.

33   Walter you like, and Annie dear,
And Dolly too, is not that queer?

WHAT WILL BE YOUR DESTINY?

FORTY-THREE ANSWERS.

———

1. Just as you think you've gained great wealth,
   Something will make you *lose your health*.

2. Your hair will be white in a single night,
   From having *an unexpected fright*.

3. *You* will enjoy a *sweet old age*,
   So kind and pure, so long and sage.

4. *You* will fall down at eighty-four,
   And break a dozen ribs or more.

5. You will finish your days *with God for your friend:*
   Who would not be glad of so blissful and end?

6. You will be *ever absorbed in books*,
   And never give a thought to looks.

7. *In peace and plenty* you will lie,
   And in the arms of friendship die.

8. You will have cause for *many tears*,
   To cloud the beauty of your years.

9   Ah, is it so? when you are old,
        You will be very poor, I'm told.

10   In the night-time *you will weep*,
        And your painful vigils keep.

11   *Nothing dreadful, nothing sad,*
        Comes to you; for this I'm glad.

12   You always will have an *excellent table,*
        And full of horses will keep your stable.

13   The Sibyl says *you'll die in Rome,*
        Which for a time will be your home.

14   Your *plenty and peace*
        Will never cease.

15   You will suddenly *die in the crowded street,*
        If the age of a hundred years you meet.

16   *You will ride in your carriage-and-four,*
        And be very kind to the suffering poor.

17   Never murmer, never care,
        You will be a millionaire.

18   *Sick at heart, and sick at head,*
        You will wish that you were dead.

19   As the might of God you see,
        Religious you will ever be.

20 To *California you will go*
    To get the shining gold, you know.

21 Brightest pleasures you will see,
    And happiness your portion be.

22 *Love will gild your joyous life,*
    Free from pain and care and strife.

23 Don't despond, and do not care,
    You will be a nabob's heir.

24 To California you will be sent,
    But will return as poor as you went.

25 *A missionary you will be,*
    Far o'er the billows of the sea.

26 It is your destiny to rule,
    And you *will keep a village school.*

27 *Balls and parties* you will find
    Alone are suited to your mind.

28 Through the vista of the years
    I see you *mourning and in tears.*

29 *A country life* at length you'll lead,
    Rejoicing in your ambling steed.

30 Far in the *wild and prairied west,*
    Your tired frame at length you'll rest.

31   *A public singer's* place you'll take,
      And a sensation you will make.

32   You'll only love *your native home*,
      From which you will not care to roam.

33   *A great pianist*, you will gain
      Bright laurels from the admiring train.

34   *A kitchen garden* you will keep,
      And sell fresh vegetables cheap.

35   To *higher virtues you will rise*,
      Until you're ready for the skies.

36   To the *city's crowded street*
      You'll direct your willing feet.

37   *In digging in a worn-out field*
      You'll see a box, securely sealed,
      Half buried in the ground;
      And therein jewels bright, and gold,
      And bank-notes, in large bundles rolled,
      Will joyfully be found.

38   *A music teacher* you will be,
      This is your tuneful destiny.

39   *You will travel* in your prime,
      And view the works of art sublime.

40   *You will journey the whole world o'er*,
      And gather relics from every shore.

41 The most of your time will be passed *on the sea*,
    But wherever you are, you will happy be.

42 On an *island will you live*,
    And nice pleasure-parties give.

43 You will spend your leisure hours,
    In a garden *tending flowers*.

ALAN SONDHEIM

living in mediaspace 68

68, azure reading, walking through the field
69, azure reading, walking down the path at a distance
79, azure reading, walking down the path a shorter distance
80, azure reading, approaching the camera from a shorter distance
81, azure reading, closer, walking down the path in winter
82, azure reading, in the woods near a small gorge, trees, streams, rocks
83, azure reading, walking by forked trees by the side of the gorge
84, azure reading, partially hidden by trees by the side of the gorge
85, azure reading, walking along a circular forest path
86, azure reading, turned slightly closer along the circular forest path
87, azure reading, walking by trees uprooted near a frozen marsh
88, azure reading, walking from a distance in the forest
89, azure reading, walking, bundled up, reading and walking

the great forest towers above azure, azure is reading in the great forest
the frozen marsh surrounds azure, azure is reading in the frozen marsh

90, reading of this world and another one before one's very eyes
91, reading of other worlds, and this one before one's very eyes

—
i will stop death by placing a tiny pebble in front of me
i will stop death's hard breathing by placing a small rock
i will stop death's approach by placing another stone
i will stop death's reading and writing by placing a boulder
a hill and a mountain, i will stop death in its tracks
a mountain and planet, i will stop death's hard breathing
—
among them or before them all, azure, a wild reading
a wild breathing, swaying, you can't hear a thing
azure's screaming worlds, and words won't come
azure's screaming words, and worlds won't come
—
death, forestall us in the forest, hinder our uneasy ways
death, caress us against moving grids and cyclones, turn our images turn our images
away from ourselves, the world erupts in desire
desire burns through the world, death save us, protect us, caress us
—
in the forest, walking across the tiniest leaves
the motions of light delicately walking and exploring the interior
of a camera
—
92, azure walking in the forest, reading
93, azure reading in the forest, walking

(UNTITLED)

Note: The text is a drastic reworking of traditional Chinese number theory as reported by George Durand Wilder and J. H. Ingram in their *Analysis of Chinese Characters* (1987).

9 writing and breathing out and breathing in, O immortal! 14 outside and foreign and beyond or outside the body and 18 reading and chanting, thinking, from the heart and two because a pair or doubling and a balance and 44 thinking, intention, and 45 thought, the wish of the heart! and the present skull! 85 see, such an eye and 87 musical theme and essay, or all the rules standing in the composition and 104 walking on the edge of the cliff! falling! disappearing! and that uneasy margin where one thing ends and another other begins and just there where i am you see the origin and 117 calling the birds and animals in their languages and names and they're calling you with their names and in their names and 121 anciently breathing in and breathing out until it has passed away and 164 sacrificing and you will try and remember the receptacle and 133 the meat and flesh of your face, nikuko! O nikuko and 188 giving you obeisance our hands above us, O trembling! 191 will continue to breathe and 238 the boat with compartments and places to carry things, floating, and a prow and an oar and 276 of opposition and division, of negation and its pull and 302 such empty leisure and what lies above our exhalation from skin and flesh, our breathing image and symbol, breathing paper

and rock and 656 being punished and knived and 723 O nikuko! calling you and exhaling and giving out through adversity, and the thin stream of air from within and 796 confined and held from within and repressed and inhaled and held, turned, stopped, named, and 42, divided and sealed

KIM PARKO

1.5

WHAT IS MEANT BY "BIRD"?

Many people when choosing an animal they would like to be will choose bird. They like the idea of flying. They believe that it is effortless. With all the effort they expend they like the idea of a break. A moment when their presence is not felt by the world and neither do they feel the presence of the world. But what if the bird's flying is difficult and tiresome? What if, as the bird descends to earth, her breath is fast and hard? And with an exhausted relief, she eyes the stable resting ground.

WHAT IS MEANT BY "GROUND"?

The ancients believed that the sky was the underside of the next layer.

WHAT IS MEANT BY "ANCIENTS"?

The ancients believed a lot of things that have been disproven by scientific endeavor. Science was created as a way to get at truth. If a theory cannot be proven it exists in an intermediary state between fact and myth. There are many such theories. Such as that of consciousness.

WHAT IS MEANT BY "INTERMEDIARY STATE"?

Bardo.

WHAT IS MEANT BY "BARDO"?

What is not meant by it? I've heard that fear is insanity. Because that is what it feels like. But soon you pass over the ability to perceive yourself. The insane feeling will not last for long.

WHAT IS MEANT BY "INSANITY"?

Recognition of the tenuous hold.

WHAT IS MEANT BY "TENUOUS"?

The substance is like water. And we all know that there are no footholds, ladder rungs, ropes, or handles contained within the water.

ELAINE EQUI

COURTESANS LOUNGING

One lights a candle.

One blows it out.

Revisiting old habits
should please use the servant's entrance

       (also known as the five senses)

and don't forget to wipe your feet.

AFTER AND IN KEEPING WITH H. D.

When I am a current
               lifted up—
can you hear eclipses' seasoning?

When you are a cure-all,
there is no signal,
               nor sorcery
trailing along.

When I am a curve-ball
               made of shelter,
O can you hear distance receding?

When you are a comment,
there is no sour cherry
trudging across sanctuary gravel.

DANIEL BORZUTZKY

BED TIME WITH WILLIAM JAMES

A heavy smoker, my friend William James, the philosopher, mowed the lawn each night wearing long pants, knee-high boots, a football helmet, and a pair of goggles.
    Before I went to bed, he prayed with me.
    "Let's round up a group of seditious waitresses," he suggested one night after our prayers.
    I answered both yes and no, for I know that love does not make itself felt in the desire for copulation, but in the desire for shared sleep.
    He formed his hands into a mouth and snapped at my crotch.
    "Don't be vulgar," I said.
    I caught myself experiencing a most incredible sensation. There are certain derivations from the norm which are more than my vegetative nervous system can handle.
    I went to the toilet to be sick.

Back in the bedroom, he was lying pretty much as I had left him: on his stomach, bent arms making a diamond around his head.
    "What shall I die of, in the end?" he asked, and looked at me as if he were expecting a death sentence.
    "An earth-moving orgasm," I said, actively taking a different approach.

"You shall die of an earth-moving orgasm," I said, for he had gone now without confession or communion since the age of fourteen, when he was a plump, rosy boy.

I stepped closer.

He looked as if he were being gagged. He laughed his little two-note laugh. His chin, his ear, I could see that his whole face was painted.

He got out of bed. He put on his goggles. He lit a cigarette. He laughed his little two-note laugh.

"The idea of eternal return is a mysterious one," James said.

"I am quite unable to deal with the pain of discovering that people hurt each other," I said.

He snapped at my crotch.

I said, "Once I saw my mother swimming naked in the ocean."

He interrupted, "And who says you have to have sex to sing hallelujah!"

He was smoking a cigarette. He was trying to do the salsa without swinging his hips.

William James, the philosopher, was smoking a cigarette. He put on a football helmet, long pants, knee high boots.

He said: "Would you like to watch me mow from the window?"

I answered both yes and no. For I know that love does not make itself felt in the desire for copulation, but in the desire for shared sleep.

It was raining. It was nighttime, and although it was not my habit, I watched from the window as he walked out onto the lawn.

He looked down, spat. He sealed his goggles over his eyes, pulled the cord to his lawn mower.

He tried to do the salsa without wiggling his hips.

"Don't be vulgar," I shouted from the open window. But it was too late. My screams could not be heard over the gristle of his delicate machine.

Experiencing a most incredible sensation, I stepped away from the window. There are certain derivations from the norm which are more than my vegetative nervous system can handle.

I went to the toilet to be sick.

RUTH DANON

CONSTRUCTION

As if
As if you had reached
As if you had reached your own
Your own gravel walk,

As if you could know what you
Needed. As if you could make some fine
Adjustments in your needs and desires.
As if you had no awareness of yourself
As a human person.
As if you had reached your own gravel walk.

In this way you were particular
About what you ate.
In this way you knew the difference between
White paper and a dark room.
In this way you made fine
Adjustments to your needs and
Desires.

(We don't need new shapes any more)

(As if you had no awareness)

(As if)

You had no awareness of yourself
As a human person.

As if you didn't need new shapes any more.

The events reported here are recent.

A fine adjustment to your needs
And desires. That blue sweater hanging
In the closest, that piece
Of bread in the white bag, those
Crumbs on the table, the green
Buds on the tree. That simple.

I want to be clear.

Each sensory moment reminds you
That you had (once)
No awareness (yourself) of
Your own gravel walk.

Recent events are reported here.

It was a kind of war between
A white paper and a dark room.

And witnesses. As if they had reached (at last)
Your own gravel walk. As if built
From the ground up, the shelter emerged.
As if everyone needed the new shapes you
Denied needing.

The shapes reported here are recent.

I wanted to be clear. I wanted
The particular. I wanted to eat.
I had no awareness of myself
As a person. I wanted to eat
Only the white paper in a dark
Room. I wanted my own
Gravel walk. I wanted a new
Shape. I grabbed the blue sweater.

The events as reported are recent.

As if. As if reached.

As yes.

STUCK ON THE STORY

The most compelling evidence is silence, flat
and new as a white fish on ice. I remember a
kind of unhappiness leading me in conception,
in foresight to an ordinary grocery at the edge
of a double wide street in a one horse town.
I'd walk the aisles of the supermarket,
everything exotic, me the passing traveler eyeing
goods mysteriously put away for the night.

There was left only the ice, the same ice
the fish had rested on, ice carrying the smell
of fish that no simple counting of hours
would eliminate. At some point they'd change
the ice, but when would that be? It never
happened though I'd keep my eyes open all
night. It's not enough to pay attention. It's not
enough to know what you want.

I was a sad little girl then. I wanted a man who
didn't want me, a fairly static structure for an
emotional life, wanting and wanting only what
isn't possible. Those white fish, they disappear
night after night, no matter how long you hang
around the perimeter of the square waiting.

That was then, in a town that boasted of a road
leading west, a town that resisted
any contemporary pattern of thought, the way
the man who didn't love me but whom I loved
would reveal himself by the stiffness that went
up his spine with every touch I'd try.

There's not enough space to tell this story, it
goes on too long. I've never tried before to stay
with it. I always flee. In conception, in foresight
I have built a house, a safe house, a place for a spy.

Only an infuriating scratch and I'm at it again, a
little sound, a little mew of a sound, I want this,
I want this. I want the place, the man, the rage. I
want the wax, the tallow, the corn. Cheese,
butter, eggs. Rags. No end to this. Time enough
to tell. I enjoyed nothing more.

HYPOTHETICAL

Okay, let's say, for starters
there's a goose in the water.
And let's say you had a little
story to tell, my my my.

        And let's say you wanted
the high road which is itself
a form of beauty.

        And if someone
were talking. And if, say,
this poem were ghostly as
two people entering from
opposite sides of a stage
are ghostly, moving slowly,
and if in their walking
there is a subtle but visible
transfer of weight.

                And if if if
two people walk without
trepidation from the opposite
ends of a room, and if something
you can't quite see happens
in the subtle rotation of hip
and arm, such that two people
face the inevitable.

         And if at the same
time this movement is so solitary
that the people remain ghostly
and so not purely formal.

         And if you could
recognize that the pain
in their hands extends
everywhere, and
if you could walk still
even more slowly across
the room yielding
yourself to ever more
various forms of revelation.

                And if you could tell
the story about the goose so that
someone would believe you

if if if then
you'd have the way out.

LITTLE TESTAMENT

Thinking about the way
this is starting to work. Something
from the outside, some sudden occurrence, startling. A woman starts out
on a slow day to run a few errands. A woman starts out
and this is no small thing, this day; these errands.
She starts out. She thinks of starting to work, and then
she thinks cold. Outside cold. And always this talk
about the weather.
What was it that the mind was thinking
while the feet were walking?

X MARKS THE SPOT

If gloves are left at a house, surely
It means something, the way going
Through a hole or arch or trap door
Means something. If gloves are not
Left at a house, that, too, means
Something, but I cannot say what.
I'm at a loss or at least I lose
Everything or perhaps it's more
Accurate to say I have lost everything,
Not believing yet that history
Has meaning. Could I enumerate
Facts in some simple way? Clouds
Are sometimes white and sometimes
Not. A tree does not always shed
Its leaves. Birds do not necessarily
Fly. You do not leave your sorrows
Behind, just because you pass through
A ring or a hole or an arch. Some say
It's new every morning, but they, who-
Ever they are, do not say what "it" is.
And what is it anyway to gather these
Small bits of information with such
Difficulty from so many disparate

Sources? The exact color of that object
Was neon green; the house was an
A frame; the disease that nearly kills
You is not known to be deadly.
You can't get away from your own
History.
        There was a small ball of yarn,
No it was thread, it was not rope, it
Was not string, and now you are naming,
Claiming, defining not what's true, what
Was true, but what you can see, with
Increasing difficulty as a harmless but
Nevertheless terrifying set of circumstances,
As when you walked into the streets
Intent on lending money at some crossroads,
As if that might hold something at bay.
        In the middle of this you confess
To a sudden confusion, how you wanted,
Say, the entrance of color. That cloud,
Remember the cloud against the blue
Sky, an azure sky, a sky worth naming
Beyond its abstract and unyielding presence
Each day. How to particularize the problem.
Is it nothing to you that I am at a loss,
That I cannot spare the cat her suffering,
Stop her from vomiting? The body struggles
Against its own obscene physicality, wanting
Some kind of dignity, or a little relief.
The animals are graceful, the animals are
Kind. They are led by people less graceful
And less kind. It's quite sharp, this impulse
To anger. The fact is anger; the sky an

Excuse; the weather is drama, the umbrella
A lie, the cold is a fact, the sweater is red.
Your shoes are broken; your heart is swollen.
                            Heart leaps up at thought
Of cloud, the thought of sky, before earlier
Accidents, before later witnesses, before
The court of law, handful of sugar, hand full
Of lemons. Remember the gloves, partly
Worn, that familiar? This doesn't leave
Me anywhere, hard crust of bread, little
Bit of food, the ecstatic disaster
Itself unnerving, dismembering; assault
Of the hands on memory, the gloves again,
Forgotten again, you go through the hole,
The arch, you go through the arch, the
Hole, you'll repeat this sentence,
You'll die trying.

BRYSON NEWHART

WIDDERSHINS

There was a time when my internal language was muddy. It was hardening into walls that I needed to attack and break down. To the accompaniment of flute music, I got busy with tonics and sumac. One morning I rigged a strappado device that was to be operated by a team of kittens. It was a contraption designed to break my own arms. It was surprisingly effective!

    In my defense, most of this starts at work where it was easy to make mistakes. Take it from me and leave the baggage at home. Instead of mincing around with sweaty hands in your pockets, walk normally. Stop setting up props and puppeting your body in an effort to open it to people that you would much rather deal with in groups. In other words, park your torso in its vesture with the hood drawn up and keep your beady black eyes on the screen. Make a mask of your face and wear it. Because the truth is, and I swear it on each of my limbs, I am not at all lying when I say that not long after this, just after the mysteriously oozing face and shocky recrudescence of hair, I learned my lesson the hard way, not just with regard to suffering through a rather difficult time in terms of rash control and my ability to respect the personal space of others, but also in terms of my job, which I lost for taking too many liberties in the office bathroom when nonconfrontational coworkers were least expecting to fillip on the light and be confronted by something frisky and bewildering, the door somehow locked behind. So what I'm saying is, next time you think it is safe to expose yourself, hunker down and consider your harness.

Suffice it to say I should have reined myself in, I should have just kept to myself. Instead, I was forced to take up reading the *Kama Sutra* on a small sunlit wall outside on the corporate plaza beside a man who slept with a backpack for a pillow, both of my arms in casts. Occasionally I would squint up at the shimmering reflective glass behind which I had left so many stunned and unwilling to even look at me. Thus perched, my swollen feet dangling above the obsessively dustpanned terrazzo—a high-traffic surface on which pumps and polished loafers struggled to make haste from the pushy broom that immediately dartled forth to whisk at the first hint of a smoldering half-sucked butt—I would spend the day complaining about the itch behind the plaster and how painful it was to hold my book; how maybe I could use a steak knife to saw slits in the casts that would free up my wrists for reading.

Meanwhile, of all the uniformed men to choose from those skittering and marching about, the sleeping man would awaken to ask a cop for the time and date. In a pother would I have to tell him to leave the nice officer alone—that, if he must know, today is the first day of fall and halfway to the solstice. Begrudgingly and with a sigh would I feel prevailed upon to illustrate with my two broken arms the angle of the earth as it orbits the sun, painfully making one cast circle the other as I explained like an exasperated father to his son how we are now tilted away from the mother of all life.

"It adds up and it has its advantages. For the next half loop we can expect an extra blessing of darkness under which to get real close to flustery individuals who can't make out what kinds of saucy activities we're up to. It's quite devilish. Thank the axis my friend. Without the tilt, no seasons. Did you know that when you look at the sun, most of what you see is the flare? Take it away and even on the brightest of days, the sun will appear no larger than the planet Venus. Ever seen Venus on the horizon after dusk? It's like a jet coming in for a landing. I used to see it in LA on the corner of Hollywood and Vine. They got some high class hookers out there."

"You talking to me?" the man would mutter. He liked to fiddle with a pair of BVDs and test their snapability before saddling them over his head. Sometimes he fashioned them as a slingshot to launch rocks at the passing crowd.

"You think I'm a cute one?" he'd yell. "That I'm fucking Jerry Lewis?"

He got a kick out of proffering a Twinkie on his palm, but before I could snatch it, unzipping his fly and snuggling it into his pants. One day while I was telling him about my dream of harvesting precious gems in the mountains of Afghanistan, he whipped out his dick with a donut clasped cherishingly around it.

"It craves the attention," he said. "I hate to see it get pouty."

On another day he opened up about his sister, a waste-management expert named Irene who lives in a jiffy bag on the Iwo Jima, a wasp class amphibious assault ship based in the jungles of upstate New York.

"She's the world's tallest dwarf," he said. "Generally we include the antlers. At seven foot five it's tough. Your oversize dwarf will get snappish. On holidays she works in a tree as a receptionist below messengers who lounge in hammocks. They operate their bikes via huggable plush remotes. Once I went to visit her with a croaker sack full of ears, desperation, and lymph node. A little something something. My intention was to bleach my hair with Clorox with the hope that maybe it would fall out this time. I figured that my last chance for quality in this life was if my hair fell out and I could glue it around my eyes, buff up my bald scalp, and mail myself to the desert in an oversized envelope. Out there I might discover a band of shrieking instrumentless rock stars in burlap jockstraps feverishly digging for snow. Men who I could nudge into pumping dollars in my face in exchange for shoes made out of banana peels. I figured they might be interested in my banana-stitched duffel bags to transport their icy treasure to the Vatican where it would assuredly fetch a high ration of plump, blistering kisses from the plushy mouth of the grand pontiff. If all went well, I figured they'd fetch me in a golden fleet of pope jets. The whole thing was based around this vision I had of us flying in formation into a blizzard of dubious friendship, rotgut booze, and unbearably freezing temperatures: a place where we might cozy up in my splendid, all-weather, banana body condoms and douse each other with buckets of good luck and moonshine."

Far surpassing my own shady interest in untenable encounters of the flesh with snaggy, unpredictable solids, clearly this man had a vision of some kind.

"Bit of a nibble on this fancy gourmet sandwich?" I might offer.

"Hey Jocko," he was known to say, interrupting me as I read. "I like to spit in people's faces. Think that's hot? This jerky likes to spit."

Fortunately, when things got overexcited, there often passed some thoughtful individual who would kindly toss a chicken cutlet on the ground so that pigeons could swarm by the hundreds, strutting and pecking from all sides as they jostled with the flabby fried skin. Will you believe me when I say that a huffy businessman, a former colleague of mine, swooped down with a turkey beak taped to his lips? That he snagged the cutlet with his beak and flew back to the office, chirping into a cellphone? Christ, the people in this town are ruthless.

Thank god for one thing. The weather remained reliable. Sometimes the sun rose and fell and sometimes it rose and fell. It worked as though on a string, flickering. When it hovered above the buildings it was hanging, everything hazy and red. The scurrying mobs slowed down and put hours in the middle of their days. They took renewed interest in flirting and rustling their newspapers. At night, the temperature was turned down and there were spotlights. They failed to single me out.

Accordingly, there came one silvery afternoon in December when I chipped off what remained of my casts and decided to embark on a series of misguided punishments that I figured I was long past owing myself. Leaving my new accomplice to his own devices, objects made chiefly of fruit, I swithered through a few luckless weeks and eventually wound up stowed aboard a waste-management barge. I was hoping to find Irene, but she did not seem to be around. What else was there to do but to go ahead and plunge headlong into the first disgusting and indefensible form of penance that was whispered in my ear by the voice? Feeling shivery and peacockish, befated for absolution, I sank to my hands and knees and began to swizzle with my tongue in a puddle of ooze. I rebuked myself for such a groveling humiliation when clearly there were plenty of razor-sharp edges I could gash my face on, but I felt sure that this nourishing blend of something chumly and unrecognizable held potential for a great lustration. Surely if I could just continue to squeege in it, I would soon become embroiled in a violent spasm of discovery of some kind—discovery of something I had hardly even begun to digest; something that might briefly splurge to the outside world via my oral cavity to be sloshingly reconsidered in the light of day before being ingested once more for keeps.

From time to time I lifted my sallow face and rakish eyes to gaze at sailors on passing ships. It did not occur to me that this might be my last chance to act charmish with a full set of teeth in my mouth.

A few months later I splashed ashore in Texas with a grinning case of the spongy gums. As I stumbled inland with arms swinging wildly in a smog of disintegrating clothing, out fell each of my teeth. Texas, my old stomping grounds, and yet I didn't feel one hundred percent. Rather, I felt forsaken and undernourished. Not only in terms of my sexual hope for copping a bosomy feel on a combative oversize dwarf, but spiritually and also healthwise. Despite its promise, the semiorganic slime that I'd been slabbering had not done much to exalt me. Moreover, despite my having stomped in these parts for years, the villagers did not seem to recognize me.

"Hey Jimmy!" I yelled, spotting the inimitable form of a Jimmy. No response.

"Hey Ricky! Hey Suzy! Hey Pat!" They seemed to be in a hurry.

Nevertheless, the twangy gibberish that they used to taunt me I was sure held the promise of hospitality. To show my gratitude, I wheeled in their direction with my clutchy arms raised high in greeting. When I got close I went to town on their clothing, administered friendly love pinches. "Hello there," I said. The people did not seem pleased. "Wanna horse around with an overexcited man in need of medical attention?" They drew away from my bloody and beseeching scurf mouth. "Wait!" I said, uselessly snapping my lobster claw hands. "Don't you want to meet my friend Snags?" I poked out the solitary, saberlike tooth that still dangled from my lips, but their fitful eyes seemed to say, "No, I'm afraid I've had an unsavory experience with a tooth." I guess I can't really blame them. After all, the snaggletooth was actually quite ravenous and would probably stop at nothing to sink himself into something, a qualmish Oliver or a Brenda not excepted—anyone, basically, who might be willing to take a chance and become good buddies. But that is not what happened. What happened was they mistook me for the type of blood-drenched man who might jump into your car with you and make lungy attempts at intimacy that could easily be mistaken, not as a normal response to the friendly glances you were clearly offering through the window as you pulled away from the parking lot, but as something else, something unseemly, something that is in fact only due to this bloody man's difficulty communicating without any teeth. What happened was they dragged me from the woman's car. They pummeled my face with rocks.

Fear is common when it comes to an old friend who you've just brutally beaten still crawling after you in an effort to grip your legs, but wanting as I did to get mixed up in something happening over the course of several weeks during which I might become flagrantly unaware of what sort of hut or orifice I was back on my feet and swaggering in, a month later it was me who was afraid. The basic idea seemed to be to see what kinds of knavish activities I could get away with and not remember a single sticky instant of before winding up utterly perplexed in the sand hills of Western Texas. One frozen morning in the desert mountains it dawned on me that I was meeting with some success. Under a hazy orange sun stationing overhead, I found myself wearing nothing but a rusty padlock chained around my waist. As I sauntered about naked like a baby just learning to walk, feeling like one of God's chosen, I remember thinking, "Surprisingly agreeable, this length of chain! I approve of it right away!"

For some reason, I decided to glue my eyes open. An attempt to lose touch with reality while staring it flat in the face? Bursting with unblinking excitement, the eyes took it upon themselves to rove in my skull like searchlights. "Dolomite!" I remember shouting when I spotted the rock formations towering above the subshrub. As the eyes peered all over discovering a lot of bones in the dirt, they provided an unperturbed landing surface for flies. But then my knees got wobbly and the eyes stopped gazing in wonder. They became indolent and fixed in shadow. To block the glare of the napping sun I covered them up with tape. In answer to your question it was office supplies—I had them. Thinking back I recall some pretty handsome eye pain.

ONE MONTH LATER:

In the underground sand cities of Lubbock, Snags became engaged in a frenzy of wanting nothing more than to snap at the sprightly bug friends frolicking inside my mouth.

I could only encourage this nibblesome madness. We passed thereafter north, through the alpenglow, and ended up in a jewelry store in New Mexico under the impression that we were in Afghanistan, harvesting precious gems, uncut sparkly little buggers. To provide a setting, I swallowed them into my stomach. It was chilling. I wound up stumbling naked through a blizzard without eyelashes. "Does the weather move over us in unison with the spinning earth? Does the earth simply spin beneath it?" In the frosty grip of these reflections, the tooth and I were snagged by mullahs. Taliban. I attempted to be polite. "Nice snowflakes you got here boys. Pretty realistic for the third world. Top-notch goats and camels or whatever the hell those things are. Mind if I sneak a tug at your beard?" In a gesture of frantic goodwill, I lunged with my chafy arms, hoping to receive a hug. These men had no love for me. Just beatings. Beatings is what they were into.

ONE MONTH, THREE WEEKS:

Ever since my days in the womb, I have dreamed of tunneling through life in goggles, my teeth sharpened for the consumption of earth, deep beneath the ocean so I might rise through dense water and float listlessly on the surface above, in extremis, enchantingly hypothermic.

On the horizon there is nothing to swim for. I escaped and that's enough. Use your imagination.

ONE YEAR:

When you cross the street as a car is rushing past, getting very close to its body, what if it slams its brakes? Could you be clipped by the remaining momentum? Because that could be very dangerous, especially if the vehicle has a hook sticking out that grabs you by the collar as the car drives on.

TWO YEARS, THREE MONTHS, FOUR DAYS, ONE HOUR:
Every 5 seconds a housefly regurgitates its food and then eats it again.
Every 5 minutes one catches on fire.

LAST MONTH:
If someone wants to eat, he eats.
If someone wants to climb up stairs, he climbs up stairs.

LAST MONTH:
Have you ever gone sledding down a hill in the same track, each time going a bit further from the hill and then walking a bit further back up? Have you ever wanted to crash your way into a wall and drop between the apartments below, just so people will hear a momentary rustling behind their picture frames and perhaps see a shirt pass the peephole?

NOW:
On Drenching Monday I finally found Irene but didn't have the heart to soak her. I figured that when it comes to a mammoth dwarf, the normal rules don't apply. Pitch a bucket of water in her face and she's bound to go nuts with the antlers.

The tree? An amusing contraption with bark on it. I knocked on the tree for service. "Anybody home?"

When the dwarf swung down I offered to wash her feet. We started kissing and it was sweet. Her mouth was filled with bugs.

"Beetle friends like butterscotch."

"Yes," I said, flooded with memories, "I had a job once too. In the East they shank you to a pole with a padlock so you can dangle upside down by your feet. It's like a flag only a flag that is really just a helpless naked human. On the ground they wear sunglasses and whip you till your eyes start to bleed. It's ruthless!"

Irene opened her eyes and flashed her mirrored eyeballs.

"Sounds good," she said. "My sunglasses are built in so I giggle a lot."

Her phone squawked like a crow as we gazed at the cool unmarked sky, soon to be sozzled with…Christ, I don't know: bad weather? rotting fruit? a migrating swarm of zygotes? Actually it was more like blueness—clearness and blueness and nice.

CYNTHIA CRUZ

WILD AND WASTE

Underneath the earth creatures have begun
To shift. A horned thing stirs behind a thicket
As blood begins to form upon its forehead.
My eyes are wide as a caged rabbit,
Dilated as a hit of dropped liquid acid.
They are not my own.
They dart about the room like a mad god
Watching. At night, with a glass eye
Dropper, he feeds me warm blue milk.
My crown burns at the places he places
His hands. I am fixed on a dark tuft
Scooping in my head. My body
Is swathed with his unbearables.
Only the skin of my tongue is my own.
At night, I keep myself alive, troubling,
Where, if they would, would they place the horns.

SEACLIFF MANOR

Seacliff Manor and those three women
frightened blank as children
pecking blind at bits of light.

I had a little dog his name was Spot.
I had a little dog his name was Spot.

Eleven years later even Schubert sounds runny.

Remember this—the bleeping white lamb,
its mouth wide open, a micro-sea in it.
Screaming, her eyes were black dots of oil.

Poppy was red as blood running, wasn't she?

Close them all shut.

Just look—the moss hills are tumbling in the sea.

ARE THEN SEEN AND PURSUED

In the forest with a rock
I hit the bones of my wrist.

Cords of voices are unspooling inside my head.

Three strange men arrive: white-gloved as beekeepers,
Removing the pleat of my body.

I dreamed the earth burned down, a bleating
Lamb hungering at the edge
Like a dark thought repeating,

If I can trace the continent of this angel,
The string will surely drag me back.

RAY GONZALEZ

APPEARANCE APPETITE

Thin bedroom street-lamp no one likes the wine chosen against postcards found after appearance accepted as the return of motionless pillows enthralled finger trace changing the rock into star hunger forgotten in the days of cracked roof tiles migratory birds blessing arrivals without droppings without seeds with water bristling eyes looking down realizing feasts replace stitches of clothing bare red petals on farthest nude image south of desire out of reach appearances necessary in time craving brown horses too swift for thin bedroom street-lamp obsession daughters restless trampled grasses wondering when appetite is encounter how many consumed answering the pursuer's liver fumes discreet taxi bathing destinies no one leaves the wine gulped against correct postcards invitations too late to disrobe.

THE MIND READER

Contradiction and the attention of stones. Placement against the vein in the mind, each thought approved, passed, taken advantage of before it is forgotten. Silence stationed to feed healthy bodies until the will becomes a talent for knowing what each person is going to do. When this source arrives, punishment is not an option, ideas and creativity already claimed, thrown back to the simple being who only wanted to think. Straight reasoning and the wilting blueberry bush in hypnotic debut, the sundial aligned with the sun, angry skeletons who failed the mental exam achieving radioactive levels the clairvoyant will profit from, without having to dig and shake bony hands. When the mind is a brain, he leaves. When the brain prefers the mind, he stays, swallows contemplation before amnesia makes a comeback and his achievements recreate themselves in time to be nothing but dreams.

DIEGO

Diego Rivera sits high atop the scaffold and watches his assistant work on the mural. His wide back and the seat of his pants expand over the thin boards of the scaffold. Diego's sleeves are rolled up and he holds a pallet of paint in his left arm, a paintbrush in his right. He has been working for two months on this mural in the San Francisco Institute of Art and things are starting to happen. Frida is spending more time alone, going off on excursions by herself, or hiding in her room claiming she is not feeling well. The other morning when he arrived at six a.m. to work on the mural before his two assistants got there, Diego saw something move high up on the wall. He retreated several yards back from the mural and looked up at the miners and high rise construction workers he painted on the top left corner. He swears one of the men moved like he was about to fall from the girders twenty floors above the earth. Diego climbed the scaffold carefully that morning, his heavy weight making it difficult to work on the narrow boards. He reached the second level and spotted a tiger coming out of one hard hatted man. Diego glared at this freshly drawn detail. Where did this tiger come from? Neither Neto or David, his assistants, would do such a thing to Diego's work. What is this tiger doing emerging from the head of the construction worker Diego labored to get right? He spent most of the day erasing the tiger and redoing the male figure. Last night, Frida took her clothes off and told Diego she was going to parade down the San Francisco streets naked. Diego sat up in bed, tired from a long day at the mural, and gave a frustrated sign. Frida spun around like a ballerina, teasing Diego to do something. Of course, nothing happened. Nothing had happened for a long time. The two slept peacefully after she quit dancing nude and came to bed. They held each other and fell asleep. One week after finding the tiger, Diego arrives late in the morning. Neto is already there, waiting for him with great anxiety. David has the day off. When Diego walks into the small gym where the mural is being painted, Neto points to the bottom right corner of the mural. "What now?" Diego asks as he sees the huge gray rat someone has painted crawling along one of the steel girders. Diego holds his head in both hands. Frida? A trick of Frida's, he wonders? No, she may hate him, but she would never touch his work. Diego bends down and studies the realistic rat that has appeared among his grand vision of industrial America. For an instant, Diego likes it and wants to laugh. He tells Neto to whitewash it. Neto nods without a word. As his assistant picks up a can of white paint, Diego changes his mind. "Leave it," he tells Neto, whose eyes bug out at this command. Diego chuckles and goes out into the courtyard of the art school building. Giant palm trees, mimosas, and bleeding heart plants line the four walls of the courtyard. Diego goes to the north wall below a classroom window and takes a black marker pen out of his shirt pocket. He moves some mimosa leaves aside that touch the building and draws a caricature of himself and Frida having sex. The black ink from the pen seeps quickly into the dry brick. In less than two minutes, he sketches the figures in their wildest coupling. He signs the rough drawing, which is only four or five inches in diameter, with the word "Rat, 1931." He straightens when he hears a couple of students walking through the courtyard. The wide leaves of the mimosa spring back into position and hide his latest creation from curious artists who might want to learn something from the great Diego.

MARK O'NEIL

ORIGIN OF BLACK FLIES

Time was when so dense and dark were these woods one could scarcely walk them. Traversing them on horseback or atop horse-drawn wagon merely a vain dream. Early hunters used dogs to take blind stabs into it, but the dogs got lost in the fecundity of the woods, ended up spilling out some time later into streams that ran too strong at that time for a dog to swim. These first dogs all died, washed up bloated on the riverbanks. Hunters and trappers canoed the rivers, walked the rapids on shore, and after years of wandering settled around lakes and ponds forming small villages, slowly chewing away at the edges of the woods. Soon, the villagers' desire for expansion of habitable territories took on the form more or less of a logging *machinery*. Ever more they pressed into the once impenetrable woods, carving pathways horses and wagons might wander, sending the rough sawn logs down the waterways, sheets of timber churning down the rapids or easing gently into clogs to be guided down the bottlenecks of increasingly turbulent flow. Loggers walked about atop these log flows with long staffs used to manipulate or *drive* the timber as one might cattle. Grids of farmland appeared, fields studded with cows; roads fit for horses, wagons, carriages meandered the habitable confines. So called permanent structures were erected, some contrived of stone and mortar, brick, but usually wood.

In the darker precincts of the forest surround there came to live an ogre incubated the whole of prehistory in the bosom of these very woods. Knowing nothing of vast expanses, horizons, having lived his days myopic beneath foliage canopies, struggling through panoplies of brush and thorn, he dwelt with his boy in a cavern of handpicked boulders textured with lichen growths as if his abode were the interior of some great, living beast. Now, the loggers brought, in excess, new smells and sounds as well as strange halos of light, sprays of spark, roils of smoke that timidly struggled against the claustral folds of night like a single candle alight within a cathedral's vaulted cavity. These haunted the ogre as he lay for sleep for they seemed, somehow, these sounds, these smears of feeble light to be organized, patterned, combined in ways suggestive of a beckoning, instilling in him a vague desire, pressing and visceral, a thirst, a hunger, to encounter and incorporate this new unknown.

So it happened that he came one day upon a stream beset by timber and glanced for the first time the forms of the drivers with their staffs, dancing upon the water. Truth is he could barely make them out among the river's spray and chaos of movement and so, forgot himself and came to the edge of the water. Spying him, the drivers maddened to panic, running against the current of the treadmill of logs until, inevitably one slipped through a crevice in the undulant floor and drifted downstream jutting here an arm, a head, then only a hand and finally a foot. He followed the course of it and discovered the driver's broken body washed up on rocks not a mile downstream. Its face was covered in a red sauce he knew to also flow from birds and crawling things and he dabbed his enormous finger in it and took a swash upon his tongue. Quickly, he pulled the thing from the rushing water and skinned it of its strangely loose, coarse hide. He found beneath something vaguely similar to a plucked bird only more loosely combined and covered in patches of a brownish-black down matted in wetness like greased fur. After sating his desire and devouring this first specimen, hunched, the very specter of *Saturn* in the grass, he found in fact that the desire was not truly sated at all but actually all the more severe. Now he knew the flavor of his object, its shape, and its signifying system—for there could be no other reason to emit odors, sounds, heat or project beckoning lights up into the night aether than some strange purposeful self-destructive bent.

Nothing else in the world went to such great lengths to make itself known. Nothing else came and went, so to speak, dipping into the woods only to vacate but always leaving behind some trace of its activities. For, as time lurched forward, the countryside, if seen from above, had become a system of Cartesian coordinates, of axis after intersecting axis in overlay upon an ever widening, infinite grid even laid invisibly where it met waters, projected upon those precincts of densest forest as if to include as points upon some meandering vector, all those inscrutable denizens, naming even imaginary or cryptid life in its bestiaries. He need only follow the traces of it to find one, those paths and roads that led invariably away from the heart of the woods to fields where other forms of life dwelt with the same dreamy somnolence that made them easy prey as well. Here he found animals nearly as large as he, white with random splotches of black and brown about their barrel-like flanks. In wooden structures mired in straw or slops, other, penned-up animals could be found—hairless boars, white and pink, overfed to the point they merely lay upon their sides just breathing and twitching their tails, and hundreds of squawking, flightless birds in cages. Of course, upon the very paths themselves the ogre often came upon a man unable to see or comprehend him even in all his enormity. How he'd pluck these up, remove their lids with one fatal swash of the teeth and turn them upside down, tipping back his head to drink them.

Once, he came upon a dead man lying splayed out, face down, upon a trail, his odors still potent, heat not yet evacuated. This confirmed his feeling that he so dominated the transitional spaces, those segues from cleared grid to becoming-mad of forest, that only the suggestion of him, perhaps merely the sound of him (he'd become in a way lazy in matters of stealth as it was so easy to pluck his new prey from where it stood) could render one dead from fright. So, he picked it up, and, flopping it over his shoulder, carried it back to the grotto where his boy waited. And when he appeared at the opening of the maw, backlit, hunched to enter, his boy came close, crowding about his father's knees, whimpering in his throat, eyes flashing between blankness and hunger. Having learned the virtues of cooked meat from watching closely his encamped prey, the ogre looked upon the last embers of their fire, the bright red coals flickering as he bent to fan them, and realizing he lacked wood, that the boy had failed to gather any, turned and flashed the boy a sneer before venturing back out into the day. The boy first knelt beside the dead man, prodded it with his finger. It was all he could do not to bury his face in its neck or start skinning it, plucking it of those coarse hairs and scrubbing away the body lice and ticks. Instead, he turned to the fire. It was important most of all to keep it going, to fan the coals, for they had no means to reinstall it and would have to stalk another camp which had become, over the years of their domination, less and less common.

As the boy knelt before their Cro-Magnon hearth, the dead man came suddenly awake, searching his person for the dagger he'd decided he would bury into the ogre's heart, thus freeing the world of his menace. It seems the world was inhabited to abundance by these hero types who devised ways of entering the ogres, behemoths of the imaginary, slicing away at them from within their soft-walled chambers, emerging reborn, with some eternal message. Thus, the dead man produced his dagger and crept, calling upon those animal powers in reserve that now flashed or echoed in his eyes. He came to full height, sprung from the shadows over the boy who fanned and blew upon the coals like some sorcerer, the dead man some conjured shade turned suddenly upon its medium. Down came the dagger in slant arcs of glint, blood spraying out from wounds opened in the boy's head and neck. But the boy wouldn't topple, rather turned upon the man who was approximately his same size, clawing at him, the dead man still flailing away with the dagger—having taken himself as paradigm—stabbing fruitlessly about the chest for the boy's heart.

Finally, the boy had lost enough blood that he was slowed and came to lie upon the spongy floor of moss and leaf rot, the dead man standing over him, panting, himself bathed in blood, thinking he wouldn't have this many cracks at the father. No, he'd have to find his heart, strike it immediately and furiously. This in mind, the dead man interrogated the body of the child with his dagger, stabbing everywhere, the child moaning and writhing beneath each query, until the dead man had gone the whole length of the child's lithe body and came finally to bury his blade in the left ankle where an answer flowed forth in a great welter of blood.

So, when the ogre returned, the dead man fell upon the giant's feet, and while the ogre labored beneath a cord of stolen wood, he stabbed away at the ankles, calling forth a blood flow as that from the beheading of a cow. The ogre came to lay beside his boy, watching as the dead man built a great funeral pyre, flames tonguing the rock-icicled ceiling, smoke flowing out the mouth of the cavern in torrents. The ogre, dying, then felt the last ghostly mechanisms of living churn within him like a system of tumblers, clicking and rattling, rubbing and connecting, until, finally, he found something spewing forth from his dry, parted lips—syllables punctuated by loud barking laughter—his voice finally unlocked. *You'll never be rid of me*, he moaned.

    The dead man chopped the ogre and his boy into thousands of pieces, crushed their organs between rocks and cast these remnants upon the fire where they warped upon first contact with the pyre's red hot center, soon generalizing into ash. This ash flaked, borne on thermal convections into the chaotic whorls of smoke until each became itself animated, forming a body of hovering particles throbbing against the confines of the cavern. They might have chased the dead man 'round the globe had he any daylight to run to, but it happened that they chased him backward into the dark abyss, the dead man finally running out of light and depths, falling prey to the ogres in droning myriad flowing into him through every orifice and he wrenching them out his mouth as if he were vomiting some vital, dark, human core.

PATRICIA EAKINS

THE OTHER SIDE

At the sign of the bleeding pole, the cutter plies his blades for our own good, to make us better than we were. *Strop strop strop* on the leather strap, then the gleaming knife descends. He cuts through the soap on our chins to nick off the hairs, he cuts through our abdomens to pull out a ruptured appendix, just in time. He cuts through a dead man's chest to pull out the heart and rides all the way over to Centralia so Mother Mary can refill the vial of the reliquary in the side chapel of the Church of the Incarnation—a favor for the nun, the least he can do—if she would just remember him in her prayers, though he is not a Catholic himself. No, a prayer is enough, ma'am, no candles, please.

    The men waiting for a cut and shave sit without speaking, each engrossed in a newspaper or a magazine, though they seem to be staring rather than reading and no pages are turning. Yet these silent men are no strangers to each other. At a livestock auction, at the feed store, at the County Fair, they greet each other laconically and swap the latest news standing side by side, each looking straight ahead, kicking the dust with the toes of their boots. In the cutter's shop the men seem to have no more voice than the corpses in the next room, or the drunken amputee, pale from loss of blood, who lies in a swoon among the dead.

He wakes with a start and cries aloud, "It's hurting me, my leg, it's hurting me." The cutter leaves Mr. Hazlitt, the lawyer's clerk, with soap on his chin and wipes his hands on his apron. He opens the door that says "Hospital" and calls over to the amputee, "You want whiskey, Johnny?"

"Please, there's something wrong with my leg," says Johnny.

"Still bleeding?" asks the cutter, eyeing the basin under the bed.

"Can't you help me? It hurts all the way down."

The cutter checks the wound where the man's thigh used to join his knee.

"Stitches holding good," he says to himself.

"It's that bullet," says Johnny. "It must be in there still."

He swears he feels the rotten meat around the bullet in the lower leg that is no longer attached to his body. Yet it hurts him, he insists.

"Drunken ravings," mutters the drover for the lumber yard, a suspicious man, wide-bodied, frank and slow, deft with horses and clumsy otherwise.

"It is the ethereal leg, the true leg, the leg of his spirit body, that he feels in his spirit heart," says Mr. Hazlitt. He holds seances in the parlor of Widow Puckett, with whom he boards. In the musty parlor, furniture shrouded since Puckett's passing, mysterious forces rap on the table, wreaths of flowers float in the gloom, a disembodied hand fondles the widow's breast, and the voices of dead children murmur from the corners.

"Oh, pig balls," says the drover.

"Where is my leg?" asks Johnny, who was shot while stealing sheep.

"Show him his leg, Cutter," says the drover.

"Dogs have eat it by now," says the cutter. This isn't true. Mother Mary has given the leg to Father John, who has shredded it in the rectory kitchen, while Bridget lay snoring in her attic closet. He put each shred in a tiny bottle tied with silken string. Then he burned the bloody apron, pulled on his cassock, and blessed the bottles. They are being sold with the candles and mass cards, a regrettable imposture, but the parish coffers are nearly empty, the paupers are a terrible drain, and the farmers and merchants give next to nothing.

"You gave my leg to dogs?" asks Johnny, shaking his head and reaching for the whiskey bottle. "Without asking for my by your leave?"

"I didn't charge you any surgery rates," says the cutter. "I took off your leg for the price of a shave. I guess I can do what I want with it."

"I can feel the teeth in my leg! I tell you, I feel them! When I close my eyes, dogs all around, their lips drawn back from their black gums."

"You go to sleep," says the cutter, patting the man's good leg. "You sleep it off. Come morning, you'll be a new man."

"New? With crutches? How the hell will I do-si-do?"

The men look at one another. The thieving Johnny is a ladies' man. What young, handsome, virtuous women there were around there, he'd won them. Hard to say what pity or patience they'd have for him now, this sly, handsome, slippery fellow who has broken engagements with the schoolteacher, the storekeeper's daughter, and the hired girl on the Barton place.

"Put them thoughts by," says the drover. "After a while, you'll get used to it."

"He said he would cut out the bad parts and sew me up."

"It was swole up black, ankle to knee, and the pi-zen was tainting your blood," says the cutter.

"Oh, no you don't! You're not going to drain my blood!" cries Johnny. He sits up quickly on his cot and struggles to stand, then faints dead away.

From his waistcoat pocket Mr. Hazlitt pulls a dainty bottle of smelling salts, which he carries to revive the matrons who swoon at seances, but the cutter waves Hazlitt off. "Let him sleep," the cutter says.

"He ain't breathing," says the drover.

"Just taking his time. His heart's fine," says the cutter, holding Johnny's flaccid wrist. "He'll be fine."

"You're sure, now?" the drover asks.

"Well, sure I'm sure. Hain't I give you my word?"

"I guess you did," says the drover. "Sure you did."

Mr. Hazlitt has pulled a watch from another pocket of his waistcoat. "The esquire will be looking for me. I get but an hour for dinner." He grimaces in the film of soap that has dried on his chin. "I say—won't you finish me off?"

There is a general shuffling, and the men file out of the hospital, back into the shave shop. There is talk of grain prices, of whether they are hiring over to the mines and what they are paying, of Rankin who got blacklisted by the railroad because he looks like that fellow Smythe who led the strikers over to Silver City. Of the hands from the Bar-Z coming into town, and them Indians from the reservation, boys getting so drunk they lie in their own vomit in the streets, so the ladies have to lift their skirts when they walk to market or to church.

In the back room the amputee has died.

The cutter shaves Johnny one last time, then lays him out with extra care. The amputee has no Sunday clothes, just a spare shirt hanging on a hook in his room above the feed store, so he is buried in that, with a jacket Cutter has, open in back. Cutter pulls it off when the viewing is over, just before the coffin lid is closed. No need for pants. For the viewing a blanket is pulled up under the hands, folded across Johnny's chest. (Cutter retrieves that, too, before the lid is closed.) Those present at the viewing see the missing leg back in place, but the shape isn't right and the leg beneath the blanket is hard to the touch. Cutter has arranged several logs in the shape of a leg. These too are removed before the lid is nailed shut.

No one knows if the amputee was Catholic or Methodist or Baptist. The divines are all circuit riders; Father John was here last week, and the Baptist, Reverend Potts, isn't due till next, so the Methodist, Reverend James, will say the prayers and pocket the coins in the hat.

In the road in front of the cutter's shop, the ladies file by the open coffin of warped, knotty boards. The schoolteacher puts a slim book of verse by Johnny's folded hands; the storekeeper's daughter, Luline McCready, lays on top of the book a bouquet of violets tied with light-shot ribbon; and the Bartons' hired girl slips a dingy wadded-up ball of cloth into the coffin.

"What's that?" asks the cutter. "What are you slipping inside there?"

"Nothing," says the girl, her face very red.

"It's her handkerchief," says the lawyer's clerk. "Bathed in tears he crosses to the other side."

"Tears and snot!" mutters the drover.

"That's it," she squeaks. "My hanky!"

"I don't want nothing with him will spoil the blanket," says the cutter. "I bet it's her drawers."

"Let us pray," says the Reverend James.

"Your drawers are wasted on him," the cutter says. He peers at the coffin resting on sawhorses, then at the girl.

"Almighty Father in Heaven…"

She has folded her hands and bowed her head.

"Be with us now in our hour of grief. Comfort us and console us…"

The girl's lips are moving, and her red face, eyes shut tight, bears a look of ferocious concentration.

The cutter's hand is stealing toward the coffin and inching along its edge…

He snatches the balled-up wad of cloth. The schoolteacher gasps, and the cutter shoots her a look. He raises the ball of cloth to his face, and his nose twitches. "If them's drawers—" He drops the ball and kicks it. It partly unrolls.

The girl opens her eyes and scrambles for the cloth on the ground.

The cutter kicks it away from her hand. It unrolls a little further.

"We are not filled with sorrow, for Jesus has told us all men shall live again. We will not grieve, for we know that our brother meets his Maker. We are not consumed by our sadness, for we know that in Paradise we shall meet our brother by and by," intones the Reverend James.

The schoolteacher has put her arm around the hired girl, who is weeping now, her hands over her eyes. "Mae," the teacher whispers. "I'm so sorry, dear."

The drover kicks the ball of cloth again. Something blue pokes out. The drover nudges it from the cloth with his toe. He squats on his heels and squints at it. "Why, I'll be—it's a little leg in a blue jean."

The girl sobs.

"A Messenger from the Other Side!" cries Mr. Hazlitt.

"Pig balls!" says the drover, then looks around at the ladies and blushes.

"We thank You, Oh Lord, for Your great gift unto us. We ask Your forgiveness and Your blessing. Fold the soul of our brother into Your bosom, and bring us peace. Amen." The minister reaches into his back pocket, pulls out a flask, and takes a deep draft. "Now what is this about a leg?"

"Little leg, like a doll's leg, but stinks of rotten meat," says the cutter. He gives it another kick, and it rolls under the coffin.

"He wanted it back," says the girl. "He hurt so. He wanted it."

"Don't go putting that thing on my blanket," says the cutter.

The girl is kneeling now. She has picked up the leg and is wiping it off. "I made the pant just like his and the boot is cut from the tongue of my own shoe, so he'd have everything he needs on the other side." She is looking up at the cutter now. "Oh, please, mister!" She holds the leg out toward him.

The Reverend James steps forward. "This is a Christian burial for a Christian man. Come the Resurrection, he'll be whole without your childish nonsense." He slaps her wrist, and the leg falls into the dust. Mae gapes at him.

The drover has taken from his back pocket a red kerchief, none too clean. He picks the leg up in it and wraps it round. He stuffs it into his back pocket. "I reckon it's a chicken leg," he mutters. "I'll burn it with the stable refuse."

Mae says nothing. Now Luline McCready is patting her hands and the schoolteacher strokes Mae's hair back from her face at the temples.

"You ready, boys?" the cutter asks.

The drover and a miner and two cowboys step forward to carry the coffin into the cutter's shop, where it is nailed shut. Then, on their shoulders, they carry the coffin to the small, dusty graveyard out near the schoolhouse. The reverend says a few more prayers and asks who would like to sprinkle on the words "dust to dust." All three fiancées step forward.

Not long after, the drover walks out on a Saturday morning in a clean white shirt with a brand new Stetson tilted back on his head. "Well, looky here!" says the cutter. The drover sinks into the barber chair. "Shave and a cut."

"Calling on the Vanderbilts?" asks a miner. He hawks one into the spittoon.

The drover says nothing.

"A shirt like that calls for a splash of Floridy water," the cutter opines.

"I ain't no pansy," says the drover.

"Then why's your collar starched?" asks a farmhand. The men leaning on the walls of the shop chortle and shake their heads. *Oh, Lord, Your mysterious Ways!*

The drover has asked for the loan of Nelly, the lead horse in the lumberyard team; he hitches her to an empty wagon and rattles on out to the Barton place where he finds Mae hanging laundry.

He takes off his hat.

Mae frowns around the clothespins in her mouth.

"I come to tell you something."

She pins a pillowcase then spits out the pins. "Nothing you can tell me I want to hear."

"It's about the leg."

Mae snorts.

"It's with him."

She glares at the drover. "Go on before I tell Miz Barton there's a tramp here making trouble."

"In the shop, at the end, while the cutter was putting his jacket by, I slid the leg under your sweetheart's shirt tail."

"Why should I believe you?"

The drover scratches his head. "S'posin'," he says. "S'posin' what I say is true."

Mae has filled her mouth with pins again.

"S'posin' Cutter pulls out the blanket and lifts the schoolteacher's book and is pulling the ribbon off the violets, and I say, 'Them things are his and the shirt too,' in case he has that idea. 'You never know, Cutter, maybe he'll come nosin' around them say-yunce meetings.' Maybe I say that. 'Bad enough you took his leg, he'll be asking for his possessions too.' Cutter is considering, maybe. And maybe I say, 'Them things are his, it ain't right to take them.' And the other fellows saying, 'Yes, that's so, Cutter, yes, that's right.' 'I'll take my jacket then,' says the cutter and goes to pull it off, lifting your lover-boy up, all stiff as he is. So I hold on to one side and pull a sleeve off his arm, and then, when I settle him back down, I keep my hand on his shoulder. While the cutter is hanging the jacket, I'm straightening the shirt and pulling it over the poor blue privates. And the other fellows turn away when I smooth it down. When no one is looking, I take the kerchief out of my pocket and slide it in under him with the little leg inside. Then I heft the coffin lid leaning on the wall and I set it on the coffin and line up the edges so when the cutter drives the nails he won't get no whiff of that rotty thing of your'n. What was that thing anyway? Before it was a leg?"

"You touched him?" The girl has forgotten the laundry now.

"I reckon so."
"You was the last—"
"Yes'm."
"May I..."
The drover waits with his hat in his hand.
"May I...touch you?"
"Yes'm."
"Which hand did you touch him with?"
"I believe it was my right hand here."
"With your fingertips?"
"Yes'm."
He holds out his big rough hand, and she places her rough little fingertips against his worn, cracked ones.
She breathes in and out, in and out, her breast heaving.
"You won't tell no one?"
"No, ma'am, I got no reason to tell a soul, none of this."
She catches her breath and looks all around.
"It were a finger."
He says nothing.
"The leg. It were a finger."
"Begging your pardon—?"
"You see that red dog lying under the house? One day that old dog come home with a human finger in his mouth. I didn't say nothing, just took the finger."
"That dog's tasted human flesh, it ought to be shot."
"He had it in his mouth, but he didn't gnaw on it none. He's a good dog."
"All the same—"
"You said you wouldn't say nothin'."
"Where'd it get it?"
"He just come in the yard with it. From out there somewhere. He's a barn dog, not a house dog. He finds what

he eats his own self, but he's a lazy dog. He don't kill nothin'."

"You think there's a corpse out there it et it off?"

"I don't know," she says. "I don't bother myself. It's done now."

"Mae!" calls a voice from the house. "You got that laundry up?"

"She'll be after me now."

Mae bends to the basket.

"You better go. She don't want me entertainin' men; she told me so when Johnny came by."

"Ben," says the drover. "They call me Ben, for Beniah."

"She'll—you—I thank you for what you did."

"Will you drive with me? Some time?"

She looks over her shoulder. "Stop by the Methodist social next weekend and one, I'll be minding her children."

When Ben and Mae are married they live in a room above the feed store, across the street from the stable, so Ben can keep his eye on the horses. He sometimes thinks about the old red dog out at the Bartons' place, wondering if the creature has had to be shot. He finds himself staring at folks' hands, to see who's missing a finger, but every man, woman and child seems to have all their digits.

"Cutter," he says one day, "you ever cut off anyone's finger?"

"Must have done," says Cutter. "So many parts I sawed off, my remembering faculty's a stew-pot."

"What happened to them parts?"

"Why, I bury 'em," says Cutter. "They's a hole out behind the shop. I throw them body parts in and throw down some lime and cover the hole back up with a stone."

"Like a gravestone?"

"Like a big old rock-stone keep off skunks and coons. I don't know but what a bear could shift it."

"What about a dog?"

"No dog I ever saw. Coyote, maybe."

"Hell's bells!"

"Them coyotes come right into town. The Indians think they got powers—"

"You suppose…"

"Too much supposing'll addle your wits. Have another chaw of Red Man. Clears the mind. Steadies the hand. Good for digestion, too."

After supper, the drover takes the evening air in the alley behind the cutter's shop, strolling and smoking. He finds no stone.

Some nights later Ben sees in a dream the cutter stirring a stew pot full of arms and legs, garnished by fingers and toes. He wakes in a sweat, sitting straight up in bed.

"Why, what's the matter, Ben?" Mae fumbles for matches and lights the candle on the bedside table. The flickering light makes tall shadows dance on the wall. He doesn't want to tell her he is still worrying the finger-leg buried with her sweetheart. He doesn't want her thinking on the amputee. He's afraid she'll take to pining for what she has lost and make that wretched fellow out to be more than he was.

"I can't sleep either," she says. "I lie here thinking about Johnny's leg. I can't remember his face, or anything about him, all's I see is that leg, and the finger the dog brung in, and how I dressed it up, and how the cutter snatched it and you sneaked it back in with John. That was the nicest thing any living soul ever done for me."

He looks into her eyes and sees a small, pale reflection of the candle flame, like a window he can't see into.

Among those sitting around the table in Mrs. Puckett's front parlor are the hostess herself; Mr. Hazlitt; the schoolteacher; and Mrs. Reverend James, who has come here behind her husband's back in the hope of speaking to her mother, who passed to the other side when Mrs. James was a girl. Ben wishes there were more men in the group. He wishes the law clerk did not wave his hands around as he talked. Hazlitt claims his hands are sensitive; when he holds them out in front of him, they vibrate.

"Someone is trying to get through," he says.

The table shakes.

"Johnny!" cries Mae.

The drover wishes he and Mae weren't here. Mae said she wanted to know where all the body parts in Ben's dreams came from; she never said she wanted to talk to the amputee.

In the corner of the room a piece of lace dances in the air. The drover can't tell if it's a doily or an antimacassar or some lady's thing he knows nothing about. "Pig balls!" he mutters under his breath.

"Marmee!" cries Mrs. Reverend James. "Marmee!" The table shakes, and there is a rapid series of crackling snaps.

"It's my baby boy. That's the lace cap he wore on his soft spot!" whispers Mrs. Puckett.

Mae squeezes the drover's hand under the table. The school teacher is sniffling. "Why are you smiling?" she asks Mae. "Can't you see that's Luline McCready's handkerchief? Can't you smell the violets?"

"The fragrance of the sweet sachets I folded into his layette…," murmurs Mrs. Puckett.

"Marmee's perfume!" cries Mrs. Reverend James.

Another flurry of snaps—the table rises and falls with a thump.

Hazlitt's hands on the tabletop are quivering. "Someone is coming through," he whispers. Then his voice changes to a coarser, deeper one. "You white men kill the buffalo. You cut the skin of grandmother earth. You bring sickness and death to the people. Where are they now who hunted from here to the edge of the world?"

"What's that redskin doing in the parlor?" asks Mrs. Puckett. "Tell him to go around to the back door, the girl will give him biscuits and gravy."

"Who are you?" asks Hazlitt, speaking now in his own voice.

"It is Spotted Horse who speaks. Of the Clear Creek people. Fallen in battle with the bluecoats, who slew my wife and my son. Watching from the sky above my slain body, I could do nothing to help them. And the land filled with your kind, even the place where my wife and my son were slain."

"Why have you come?" asks Hazlitt.

"I have heard my wife calling, the wail of my infant son. No one washed their bodies. No one dressed them in new deerskin. No one built a fire. The smoke of their passage did not rise. They wander, and I look for them, to show them the way to the other side."

"Snow!" cries Mae, pointing to the corner where the lace has been floating. White feathers are falling, turning slowly in the dim light.

"We, too," says Hazlitt, "search for our loved ones. You who have wandered the realms of the living, looking for the shades of your loved ones, can you help us find those we love, who wander among the shades?"

"Burn the bones," cries Spotted Horse, his voice seeming to come from among the feathers. A brown hand materializes in the air and is raised in benediction or farewell, then vanishes among the feathers that continue to fall. "Burn the bones," whispers the spirit. "Farewell!"

Now there is a great clattering under the floor, as of bones struggling to rise. Ben pulls up the tablecloth and the company gasps. Lying under the table is the red dog from the Bartons' place, its lips pulled back in a snarl.

When the company looks back up, a leg hangs suspended in the corner of the room, dripping blood on Mrs. Puckett's turkey carpet. Mrs. Reverend James faints dead away. Spotted Horse refuses to rematerialize. The drover is suspected of signaling an accomplice by pulling up the tablecloth. People in town eye him funny when he passes. The schoolteacher rides into Centralia to telegraph the marshal. The drover hightails it out, riding Nelly, which makes him a horse thief. Mae waits for three years with only the Bartons' wandering dog for occasional company. She supports herself by sweeping up for the cutter. She prays every night for the drover's return, and for Johnny's, too.

At the end of the three years, she gets a ride with a rancher and his wife to Centralia, where she marvels at the gingerbread decoration on the houses and the mansard roof of the town hall. She shows Mother Mary the stigmata she has made by digging her fingernails into her palms. She is accepted as a lay sister, and she covers her hair. Her work is the work she has done all her life—washing dishes, sweeping the floor, feeding chickens, weeding the garden, emptying slops. She memorizes a great many prayers in Latin, of which she has no understanding, though she likes to say them in the side chapel near the reliquaries. It comforts her to be in the presence of sanctified flesh, barely visible behind tiny, cloudy windows. She forgets all about Johnny and his leg. She forgets the drover too. When the cutter rides into Centralia to propose marriage, she refuses.

MICHAEL IVES

THE FOUR FINGERS OF THE LEFT HAND
for Janet

I.

The boat was moored in a cove. Mother and father had gone ashore and left my sister and me on board to wash the decks. One of them had thrown a kerosene lamp. We were rinsing down the cockpit when both of us saw a woman rowing very quietly in an old dinghy away from a clump of junipers. My sister climbed to the mast and held the halyards away from it and asked if I could hear a faint metallic clicking. "A little," I said. We tried to look busy when the stranger pulled up alongside and drew in her oars. My sister said hello. The woman was very old and wore a torn blue scarf, the corners of which were drawn together under her chin with a gold ring. There was a strange wrinkle above her upper lip. One of her eyes was clouded over. On the forward thwart of the dinghy there was arrayed, all open and playing, a row of music boxes, more than twenty. Some were made of wood, others covered with satin. One had a blindfolded ballerina turning in its center. When her oars were stowed, she pulled two large water fowl from the bottom of the dinghy, one in each hand, and stood up and asked us, "Which of these is your father?" "My father is a man," I said to her. "He will be," said my sister.

II.

"If the stars fall, will they burn through the sails?" I asked my sister. Mother and father were asleep below. It was one o'clock in the morning. By compass we sailed on a following wind around the shoals known as Cross of Mouths in a curve whose name we could not pronounce, though we knew it to be infinitely long. Orange and red panels of the spinnaker through which the moon shown cast across the deck a color we knew only as "one o'clock and nearing the Cross of Mouths." When we passed into the broad shipping channels, my sister reached inside the companion way and switched off the running lights. Soon we were hedged round by limitless banks of cold time. The warmth of our passage through them felt like the trail left by a half-articulated question. Later in the night, leaves began to fall on the decks and into the water on either side of the boat, maple leaves, illuminated by moonlight as they fell out of their darkness. We were hours beyond sight of shore. "But where are the trees?" I asked my sister. "These leaves are real," she said without looking up from the compass. The light of the binnacle threw her eyes into shadow. "These are the only true leaves there could ever be."

III.

It was late March. The boat was up in its cradle. One half of the bottom had been sanded for painting. On the other half, my sister and I drew pictures with chalk. She drew horses, many of them, all from the same angle. I put plus signs between the horses and then drew an equals sign after the fifth horse and then a boat. We both laughed. She drew a boat under a division bar and a snake to the left. "Vessel divided by snake equals…" "Mom," I said, and we laughed even louder. We played catch with a tie-dye colored kick ball. A tall man we didn't know with one leg shorter than the other came up and wanted to see it. My sister looked over at me then turned to give it to him. He snatched it out of her hands and held it out away from his face. He looked at it and looked at it. We grew frightened. Suddenly he spat to his side and yelled, "This ball curdles my blood," and hurled it over my head and turned and limped toward a station wagon where a woman waited. She was waving to me and pointing in the direction the man had thrown the ball. When they drove away, I turned and went to look for it. I walked into a large patch of wild carrot between two immense and aged cabin cruisers rotting away in their cradles. It was like entering a gorge to go between them. In the shadows I parted the wild carrot and tall grass. I found half a ladder and an old block with cracked wooden cheeks and sheaves rusted in the swallow. The hulls of the cruisers curved and rose over my head. There were flies. I slapped one hull and stepped sideways and slapped the other. Under the rusting screw of one of the hulls, there lay, half in sun, half in shadow, a dead deer. Someone had cut an elaborate flower shape out of a newspaper ad for boys' clothing and then cut a circle out of the flower's center and placed it over the eye of the deer. Rain had molded the paper to the shape of the deer's head. Dimes were inserted between the lips of the deer in such a way that the dimes looked like teeth. I flecked maroon paint from the bottom of one of the cruisers as I stared at all this. Chips of paint fell onto the deer's haunches. My sister came up from behind and was silent. After a time I kicked the deer hard. One of the dimes fell out of its mouth. My sister said, "Did you just kick the deer?" "You *saw* me kick it," I said. "That's why I asked," said my sister.

IV.

I had not yet finished dressing and already too many people were streaming into the house. I knew this without leaving my room. When I ran to the top of the staircase, my sister was already there. She had made a pouch for her shell collection by gathering up her nightgown in the front. One of her arms was through the sleeve of a sweater. The rest she was pulling over her torso as though readying to leave. "You people look too much like fire coming into the house like that," she said to them, though they gave no indication that they heard her. The sound of her voice reminded me of a marble we had buried near the river, thinking it looked too much like an eye. I ran back to my room and took down the poster of North American fresh water fishes and rolled it up and put on my sneakers. There wasn't time to look for the last thing. When I came back to the stairs, my sister had her sweater all the way on. The shells were arranged in a perfect square on the floor, and she stood within it looking out of a window toward the bay. I told her I was ready to go. "We're already there," she said.

THE SKEPTIC'S ANATOMICAL PARABLE OF SIGHT AS AN INFINITE REGRESSION

Gatherers, or eaters, vintners, even sculptors, of light, they have been called, the eyes—lumenivores…sight, *the exquisite hunger of the self*…but these extravagant folkways, by an easy and rustic anatomy lesson, are quickly disposed of, for there is little to vision aside from a slab or great mortarwork stele (in opus incertum)—of tremendous height, I'll grant you—with fragments and powder of it broken and strewn at its base— thus the vaunted retina—Rome and ruin of the truth—and, for that matter, whether within or without the skull, what difference? A chauvinism merely, this within and without, the vulgar distinctions of a surveyor—yet, forced to conclude, let us with policy join the mob and situate it within, as the psychological epoch demands: that the matter be concluded *once and for all*, and that it be within, that the powers, the receiving powers, the individuating, sovereign element—to speak liberally, the sight…that in essence, all agencies of sense, of self-making, be located within, and, for the sake of brevity, and as not to importune the precious *untrammeled will*, perfect and absolute self, node of intention, governor, etc., we will, if only for the record, put the sight properly within the skull—with rudest carpentry house the jewel. Idiots!

At the lower interior reaches there stands in the dims and waste a witness, a groundling—vermin if it please you—squinting above him into the starless vault, following the stele heavenward as far as is visible, into, as the poets say, *shadows of neither evening nor unnatural day*, to a height at which one in dreams rises, but in waking deems specific to the unattainable, *close glooms of the upper skull*. From across a narrow chasm two portholes—oculi if you wish—of Leonardean circumference, in horizontal attitude, bathe the empyrean reaches of our slab with the vague commotion of external fact, and while pulling a dim profusion of ivy from the chinks in its mortar, shed for our witness sufficient light to behold one further marvel: hung, or in some manner suspended between access of light and immemorial brickwork, two spherical masses, half illuminated, half nearly imperceptible. It is as accurately said that they float—a stationary hovering, two rippling moons, though, with adjustment to the dimness, it becomes plain to him ratlike below, that they are each a cloud, a swarm, multitude of complementary and fleeting vectors spherically resultant… some, though never so many as to harm the collective endeavor, repairing to the ivy bower to roost and gender, some winging westward toward their extreme Gibraltar, but of what these trailing globes are composed the witness is always as yet unsure. All that can be ascertained is the swarming, and that it kindles in him, who strains to see, the rudiments of his own attention. We might as well, for all the eyes may deduce, remove ourselves to *his* skull and find at its base, there among the broken stones and first shadows, another who stares above at the dim prodigy of two perfect but swimming spheres. Yet a third trepanation within the witness of the witness would only reveal the same composition…more witnesses, more steles, more spheres… always the unscalable monument, the silent watcher, always the scarcity of light and the inscrutable orbs before it—of birds perhaps, swallows to hazard a cleverness, viz. as of the light, a darting species to be approximate, birds at any rate, or possibly bats, and extraordinary darters those, offering over swallows the distinct advantage of such additional symmetry as to place vermin both above and below, a verminous antipodes, the self, or *batting about of light to ever more futile uses.*

Addendum: Bats are not, properly, vermin.

KENOSIS

I was taught that the shape of a body lives longer than a body itself. Likewise, I was taught to build at the shore, when the disfigurement of living was complete, whether from age or disappointment, a simple enclosure. I built mine of bleached drift and rootwood near where a newly risen stream gave out into the lake. Syringes and tampons shifted in among the leaf-litter at its bottom, darkened in patches by the shade of sumacs growing along its banks. I pulled up the roots that ran into deeper water and cut through them with half a scissors. My hand bled as I bound the drift with the root, and there was a willow over me whose eye I caught unraveling in a bee. As I walked to the store to buy lard, I thought of what it would be like to walk inside a bee. When I brought the lard to the counter, the grocer was staring at me. "God help us," he said as he passed the canisters over the scanner. "Yes, them too," I said, and gathered up the lard.

    Since I was borne out of the only place into this one, I pissed all over the enclosure and then plastered the interior with lard. It was very hot the day I went for good into the enclosure. There were cones under my face that had begun to drill toward a mussel somewhere in deep. For most, the enclosure would have looked like an unreadable letter until I crawled into it. Of course, once inside and no longer able to distinguish where my skin ended and the lard began, and after that, what was lard and what stick, it became readable enough for a boy and a girl to come up to the side of the enclosure and for the girl to say, "I'm going to touch the christ child."

"Mom said not to touch the christ child," said the boy. "She said not to *trust* the christ child, so I'm going to touch it instead," and she put her hands against the enclosure. I could feel my eyes growing too far distant from one another ever to be considered a pair again.

MARK DeCARTERET

ode to antarctica

yeah, south of south
snow & cold & all that
so happy how we mouth
your formations lowest land
maybe you have penguins
& the light playing
all by its lonesome

title

in a field
familiar
in every
way
but the birds
flying in
forced
exhalation
unlike
any I've
seen
then it's winter
I'm a fountain
of trembling
in a house
w/white walls
& a lady bug
struggling
to get back
red again

MANDEE WRIGHT

JUXTAPOSITION

This is an account with no dialogue.

Back in those days, we were unaware, and we unintentionally spawned. It was half-hope time—garden greenery wilted under the summer heat and the city stunk from it for months on end. It didn't rain all summer. We conserved through ordinary traits, washing our hands from gathered water in pots in the sink, watching our plants turn white from radiation, showering together like stoics but to no avail. Everything dried up anyway. A small jungle gym rested in a gravel pit outside our bedroom window and every afternoon a red-shirted boy swung for an hour, becoming breathless, and then he'd slip away, safely, into his envelope of a home, somewhere near mine.

Students—we said it to adults and parents, but we didn't realize what it meant. What were we studying? Some vague liberal arts motif that involved reading and writing and skipping class and avoiding professors' menacing glances—but studying? That fell in with the forgotten envelopes, like the boy's. We looked at books and passed them around, underlining key phrases that maybe had some shred of doubt that rode along with them, index cards flying around like paper doves, title, author, and the quote waving goodbye on a term paper. Bye-bye, they said. They chirped.

We were broke and bored. I gave myself over to them. So did he. Our net worth would skyrocket to $5,020. There would be no confessions.

Juxtaposed on two operating tables, a Mexican woman and I held a conversation before I would fall victim to anesthesia. She clutched her abdomen like a paper sack about to flail into the wind, being lost to oxygen. Paper dresses rip more easily than expected. I wiped my fingers nervously along my sides, leaving behind greasy inklings like some squid had found me, found mine, found my heat, and refused to go; it couldn't decide. Were the woman and I twins? They left us there together.

My glasses vanished after my operation. One minute they were there, laying on my bedside table and then they slipped away, sealed up in something we couldn't see. I, myself, couldn't see. He told me I looked as if I had been hooked like a fish and thrown back with the others, just a tiny incision etched pink below the slope of my stomach, contrasting with green tones. My glasses were green.

The five thousand dollars scattered quickly, like the doves—and also like my glasses, we didn't know where it all disappeared. We had already established that this was some sort of equal contribution, but between the two bathroom sinks his hair littered the countertop more than mine ever had.

My hook mark was barely visible except in fluorescent lighting, lecturing on the right side of me. I couldn't slip for fear of sliding over and gutting myself—spilling myself out and unveiling other things still covered. He knew I was scared, scared of being hooked again or losing others so he put a yellow Band-Aid over it. We had the same thing in mind.

August was no kinder than the previous months—we were drier than moths and skin flakes flew everywhere when

I scratched my neck. The skin surrounding my incisions crusted over pink and purple; diseased like some dead reptile (a green iguana I had once had named Gin). I began to look forward to the courses of the fall: rain and schoolbooks, pregnant women in some other cities, clicking their tongues in excitement.

Other languages have a complex system, a precise, needle-point-thin definition for one word that maybe will appear in one instance in one sentence of someone's conversation over the phone, but that word exists; it circles around in some universe of others, always ready to be found, extracted. This language leaves us half-filled, and even then, you have to string together some sketchy adjectives to get them honest. My queries are never answered, my words are left vacant, and I struggle to think about what I was thinking about.

Whether one recognizes it or not, there is a word, a verb, for when one's glasses fog over from moisture. This verb pertains only to the fogging up of glasses, spectacles, not of windshields, or windows, or containers of wind, likewise, vice versa—eyes, coverlets, glasses. Those apparatuses. Mine were missing. They were green.

I found my glasses in late September. They were inside my hospital slippers like some cockroach. It rained that day and I havered like I had never havered before.

This, as I stated earlier, is an account with no dialogue, and I am about to change my mind. Dialogue is about to sprout across the page—and not only that, but unimportant, irrelevant dialogue.

Here is the scene:

He and I sat adjacent to each other, juxtaposed like two nuns, I—reading a cooking magazine, eyeing the slick exterior of a Christmas ham pasted across the front cover.

He poked me in the back, his symbol for something meaningless about to spill out of his mouth:

—That ham. It looks like someone I know.

I mumbled something to the effect of a prying utterance, ending it on a high note, implying an edge of question.

—Yeah. This guy I once knew—he had a greasy face just like that.

Dialogue such as this, it doesn't say anything. He wasn't communicating to me the way humans do, through signals. Alarm clocks can go off, making sounds that repeat themselves over and over again until there is a response. The alarm does not think, it has no consciousness—it can only think to make that sound, the alarming sound. Sounds were falling out of his mouth, but they were muted by the fear of being alone. Thoughts—they like company, but they sometimes cannot be spoken. He spoke to me through dialogue, but I couldn't understand him.

I never really knew him through dialogue; I never really knew him in one moment, like how you can stare at your hands in front of you and know exactly where they go and where they came from, and what their use is. You know the lines of them, the way they slant in the air in that single solitary slice of one day. He wasn't like my hands, or my glasses, or any ordinary thing that I know in one moment of one day, or maybe in one piece of one dialogue between myself and a woman on the street corner—he was a network, capillaries that spread throughout my mind that could not have possibly existed in only one moment, but an hour, a day, infinitely, like the weight of my body that I forget I am carrying around.

My mind stopped working in words and regressed to the language of pictures. I thought of myself as one of those amphibians who carries her eggs on her back. If only I could carry them there, exposed in the daylight. The surgeons wouldn't have had to cut me open that day—they could have plucked off a few, fresh and pearlescent, and instead of being left with me who would ignore them like some scab just out of reach to scratch away, given away to women who wanted to be pregnant.

Those classes began again after the rain and he and I were forced to communicate through short, stabbed notes on scraps of paper left on the kitchen table. Maybe it's just some terrific sickness that we all have where we think fall was created for ourselves. I saw a bird today while I drove, hundreds of butterflies float past my window shading green sunlight and I'd realized the birds, the butterflies—they're just rotting leaves, brown and green and that this heartache wasn't meant for me or anyone else for that matter.

Nothing changed for him and me. The papers began to crowd my dashboard, razored with red ink and barbarisms of time between appointments. A comment, she wrote. This is ridiculous, not even a punctuation mark to end that despair. But, then I remembered—despair never does end.

I asked him, and he agreed my stomach looks swollen and uncomfortable.

We also agreed that the most disgusting phrase in all of this language is this: "She will make babies someday."

The leaves had been flooding the streets and I recalled back to the days of conservation; how those hand-washings had seemed so lavish and decadent—it was strange to me that the gravel in the playground was now always sopping like some fibrous cereal. The boy in the red shirt had gone away from us, and I wondered where he went—if he, like that unknown embryo, was growing in somebody else's stomach. She will make babies someday; I will not. Someone else will make them for me, and we will have unintentionally spawned. He didn't know it yet, and neither did I for that fact, but our dialogue had been lost into the baby that was growing. It was talking to itself inside some woman whom I did not know, relaying that dialogue in the gelatinous placenta, realizing it would never speak to the world. The boy in the red shirt, maybe he wasn't gone, but he always would be as long as he wasn't swinging where I could see him. As far as I knew he was dead. He was a dead boy to me, draped in a red cloth to match his shirt that had been long forgotten. That jungle gym outside our bedroom window; I grieved over it. It wasn't a labyrinth of steel held together, it was a headstone where so many red-shirted boys had been lost. They were not counting the moments, the particular second when it is appropriate to go flying off the swing; they were waiting to be reborn into somebody who would ultimately hate them.

It was as if my abdomen had been stolen from me quietly in the night—that round globe had been developing on some other woman's stomach. I imagined a retarded boy named Otis coming from her womb, growing up to have a constant cowlick and a long string of drool hanging out the corner of his mouth. She'd have to remind him to eat his corn, to brush his teeth, propping his head up for family photographs, his eyes flailing down to the corner of the photograph like he's eyeing some cat or a disturbance in the shadowed section of the room.

And him, that man who I began to relearn through the papers and the rainy nights that erased us both, tricking us into believing that something new had been uncovered, he knew nothing of it in the most disturbing of fashions. Reading through the entertainment section of the newspaper, commenting on some four-star review—he didn't know; he had no idea what we had done, how our spawn was stretching out, meiosis, mycosis, capillaries that I knew him through, they were growing inside somebody else that would form another red-shirted boy, but one whom I would not recognize. He knew nothing of anything in the most disturbing of fashions; the way that ham was reiterated ridiculously through his speech, the way no matter how hard I tried I would always look up from my plate at breakfast and find myself alone, the newspaper rumpled like an abandoned sleeping bag, those four-star reviews left and forgotten.

I felt that pregnant woman in some other city's remorse. She would give birth to an impossibility that would hate her through dialogue.

I slipped away from him that fall, like my eggs had slipped away secretly to that vial, hurrying from that gelatin mold of an ovary. Every morning I would approach those big wooden school doors, seeing pink flesh peek out from hats and mittens, and it would disgust me. Breakfast would always revolt, finding its way up my esophagus and I'd have to leave that institution. I couldn't stand people's eyes on me, their flesh pulsing behind their eye sockets, the way a professor would open their mouth, strings of saliva stretched across their incisors, their lips stretched up into the light revealing their slippery red tongues. It made me sick, all of it. I couldn't stand to see their yawning cheeks and yellowing skin—I would always envision one of those photographs of an enlarged mosquito perched on some innocent's forearm; how those skin cells seemed as large as god's, immense holes that could eat you alive while you slept—those cells were out to get me, their dead selves falling all over my footprints.

So I'd bicycle home, flopping on the couch, entertaining thoughts of a better life, but ending up falling asleep every time, my pillow sliding out from under me. I nodded my head, balancing between the thin line of sleep and awake, dreaming of myself walking through the city, carrying my azure coat behind me as if someone were inside of it, droplets of water following us, crystallizing in the air and then falling to the ground and breaking, the beautiful dissonance of glass shattering, the waves lapping against the pavement. The dream felt like some life to which I should have belonged. Had I been avoiding the sky? Clouds floated by overhead, tinted blue, like some strange sea anemone staring out from its display case, floating by, and ignoring me.

It was as if I was following something I couldn't—maybe my coat, or air, or the city itself, the lines of my frame rippling through the water parading through the downtown alleyways, women wading through the streets pulling out their hair as their babies floated away from them.

He would never return on time; the refrigerator stood open, the bright colors of condiment bottles gleaming in that beautiful light. He would arrive, his coat falling to the floor, heavy and dumb. He would find me, and touch my shoulder lightly. I'd shudder at his touch—his hand, slimy and pink, leaving behind a trail of skin cells on my body—skin cells that weren't mine, which bothered me the most. I felt grateful I'd given those eggs away; I couldn't bear to have his sperm in me.

I could tell by his facial expressions that I had started to bother him, just as he bothered me. He was one of those tiptoeing silent types who always listens to music on headphones and never shuts any doors, but rather, allows them to quietly journey to a crack in the doorway. I'd rummage through our kitchen cabinets, slamming them shut, pushing drawers closed violently—I could hear his mind squirming as he sat on the couch watching me. I made noise whenever I traveled, shuffling my feet down the hallway, flopping on the bed, making the mattresses groan in protest. The louder I was, the quieter he became, like he was shrinking back, retreating from my awesome power, as if I had a hold of his hair as I marched around; soon he would just be transformed into my lap dog: quiet, sitting at my feet like a rug.

We hardly ever spoke because my voice would always crescendo over his, no matter how hard he tried: he'd be on his knees, my stomach in his hands, and maybe he could hear those two heartbeats that would always outweigh his.

Usually conversation breaks situations like this in half, but we said nothing to each other. We'd tear the sheets in half at night trying to decide which one of us would conquer the other. If I could have remembered what songs would make him give himself over to me, I would have happily played them. Light from outside leaked onto his head beside me—it was as if he was only created for hair to grow, the strange forests of thin wiry hair that grew more and more grotesque the closer my eyes came to his scalp. I waited for him to stop breathing.

Before this I had been the one who always came back. But I knew that I was going to be the one that stopped breathing in the night, not him. He stayed alive. I slid over the ice into my car and drove off into the darkness, the trees framing the night like some exclamation of smog, out of the city, where only the barnyard lights flood the streets. Cows numbly breathed in the darkness; they stared back at me, kicking up dung in the feedlots, the dull flame of my lighter cascading over their pupils. They moved across the earth, stumbling in the same fashion, as I struggled to gain composure while walking through playground gravel. I thought of him and the child as I leaned against my car, staring at the movement of the cows' bodies—I thought of him, and I couldn't decipher, I couldn't figure out which personality I had fabricated, which one had been the original: myself, or him.

RAPPEL

SENOJ

His being has merged with the rhythm of complaint, nothing else gets played. The screen won't latch, the cup broke (he dropped it), the goddamn air is too *salty*. The rhythm is so consistent and numbing that time is no longer distorted by it. Complaint drives him from chair to couch, it's verbally constricting but it keeps him moving, gesture by gesture, through something called life. He's earned this rhythm—but can he hear it? That isn't the question. Is he listening? That isn't it either. With three decades of retirement behind him—thirty years of decrease and neglect—what is the relevant question?

    Senoj is exactly alone. No questions pull his mind into shape: his mind drifts, he no longer follows. He forgets to eat dinner but remembers his bath. He sinks into warm water and the drift takes over. Finally his state of complaint recedes so far that his agitation ceases. His thoughts disintegrate and merge with oblivion. He veers into the final tolerance—stops breathing. Something snaps and he's gone.

But no. He fluctuates. The gravity of inverse time catches up, pulling him back from the finish. He is returned intact to his life, though facing the opposite direction.

    He doesn't notice.

Day follows night and the juice of complaint flows again, nourishing as milk. The ache in his knees diminishes—but a pain in his neck returns. His watch reappears, but not his glasses and suddenly the radio is blaring. The couch where he sleeps turns lumpy and smells, but he finds he can climb the stairs. He returns to his bed which is just as he left it, and at breakfast Helga the housekeeper reappears. The old routine starts up again, everything as it had been, is again. He notices sirens in the dead of night, hears planes overhead, goddamn cat in the alley. Old annoyances fit so well he forgets there were days when he had heard nothing. His sphere of maneuverability increases—it should amaze him, but he takes it for granted.

For the next thirty years his natural resources reknit him into workable form. His muscles fill out, teeth return, cups that broke are unbroken.

One day he puts on a suit and tie, takes the train to the city. There is nothing that isn't familiar. With great ceremony they confiscate his watch, then the office once his is his again. He sits down and animates some papers. Now that he is in command, his dissatisfaction can spread. He is surrounded by people to blame and the act of blaming releases toxins that Senoj would have had to swallow. He feels fine. He feels great. He trims a cigar and lights it. It is natural now when a question is asked that *his* words have priority. His signature alone can make things happen in the city he owns through his plate glass window.

Nothing prevents him from looking ahead and seeing the line of impending demotions that will lead him back through the years to the stockroom, all the way back to college—but no. Senoj doesn't look. He's so accustomed to seeing nothing ahead that he continues to see nothing. This is, of course, his prerogative. Seeing is a personal decision, though highly modified by cultural standards: those who see too much will despair; those who see not at all will trip. It is only in dreams that Senoj veers off-center and sees—anticipates, with anger and alarm—the grind of working his way back down, becoming less in the eyes of others—less competent, less confident while knowing, deeply, that he'll never be any better. It's only in dreams that he knows where he's headed—dreams from which he awakes.

He wakes now with a sense of others—he vividly imagines a son named Harold, he imagines a collie, he imagines Hannah...Then Harold re-enters Senoj's life, with a single phone call Harold is there. He has a rasping cough, but he's fine, he insists it's nothing, stop worrying for Godsake. Here's Harold's wife Mia and Mia's brother and her nephew and someone he never knew. Then Hannah his daughter slips into the house, she wants to stay over and he doesn't say no. She brings him a jar of fresh peanut butter, brings cartons of books and suitcases to the attic. Her life is quickly entangled with his in a way that distracts him from his fourth demotion. Likewise his son leaves more things at the house, for Mia has vanished along with her brother. And although Senoj has little to spare, both Harold and Hannah prod him for money. Then suddenly Helen his wife reappears and Harold and Hannah retrench themselves as if they had never left home.

Distracted now from the pulse of the world, Senoj is caught in the web of family, and he has little left over. For as soon as Harold and Hannah move in, they are restless and want to move out. Hannah is sullen or outright angry and Harold is an arrogant barbarian. Senoj forbids them to drink. He demands explanation for their erratic behavior and tests their excuses for flaws. It's a time of slammed doors and broken mirrors, of whispers or shouting but not much between.

But just when Senoj decides he can't bear it, Harold and Hannah retreat into fantasy. Leaving the common world, they play. They pretend to be prince and princess. They pretend to be baby bears and bunnies, tables are caves and the cellar a dungeon. They allow themselves to be fed, finally, to be read to, sung to and coddled. And Senoj himself gets down on all fours, he turns himself into their horse. He coos. He clings to them as if he knows that nothing lasts forever. This gives his affection depth. He has no complaint, here at this junction, in the sanctuary of his family.

Then Harold disappears and Hannah follows, and their faces and voices are lost forever. Senoj is alone with his wife.

Alone. The house is too large, they sell it. The new house is tiny but eventually it's perfect; it is exactly what they want together. And Senoj finds Helen increasingly desirable although she has lost her confidence and has no discernible skills. Senoj feels his own solidity through her—he is going to fall in love, and he knows it. He feels it approach and desires it. Falling in love from the opposite direction is no less seductive, no less profound: experience is always experience.

But coming to the time where he first meets Helen, Senoj becomes confused. The content in his psychic channels turns volatile and, as if he perceives what is going to happen, he clings to her, he is haunted by her—yet he can't forestall her impending erasure. At the point where his life intersects with hers, they'll become oblivious, entirely, of each other. He won't have even her name to call out, because he hasn't met her.

Senoj then returns to school, and he's relieved to know what he is doing. He has a lot to unlearn. He is required to put down on paper all the facts of a given subject—facts he must now forget. Vast networks of interconnected material must be dismantled, fragmented, dispersed. Unlearning, which is specific forgetting, proceeds page by page, test by test. Finally it will seem natural to know very little without realizing exactly how little.

Other things concern Senoj at this point, he is awkward and unsure of procedure. He's thwarted by mistakes and miscalculations, he can't hold a bat, he forgets how to whistle. Coming to childhood from this direction, Senoj struggles to find a position. He fights to hold on, but he's forced to let go and the world he had known turns vague.

Senoj is a simple, lively being, primitive, forgetful, unresponsible. He hears rumors from his cousins and playmates regarding his body and the body of his mother—terrifying rumors—he refuses to listen—that when he is small as Sunday's chicken, lacking the wit and the strength to struggle, that his mother—but he refuses to listen, goes off and plays by himself.

But despite the terrifying rumors, he's increasingly drawn to the presence of his mother, to her body warmth and sheltering size. He wants to stay in the room with her, he wants to be on her lap, in her arms. Being separate from her is unbearable and she—she indicates she feels the same way. The gap between them narrows. There is nothing in the world for him but her, and likewise for her there is only him. When the attraction reaches maximum intensity, she is unable to resist him. She pulls his tiny body close and sucks him in through her vagina.

She locks him inside her; it is night.

Does he feel himself beginning to dissolve, like a tablet in water until he is nothing? His *nothing* now splits into two complications, each taking a separate direction.

PETER MARKUS

GIRL

We walked through that place where town used to be, where now there was just a river muddily flowing. We were the three of us, here at the dead end of the road, two brothers with Girl in between us, our hands hooked in that crook of where Girl's elbow made the shape of a sideways laying V. Here, where town used to be, now, there was just the river and a hand full of shipwrecked buildings watching over where the muddy waters continued to still flow, so many doors waiting to be opened, windows without people to look through them, each rust colored brick trapped by the weight of what held it in its place. Town was the place we used to go to with our mother or father when our mother or father needed some little something from the town hardwares store where our father used to talk nuts and screws and fixing things with old Mister Higgerson with the one leg that was lost in the war who stood there and listened and nodded his head and sometimes, after our father was done with saying what he had to say, Mister Higgerson liked to tell us how it was that he lost the leg that was missing from where it used to be on his body. What I remember most about what he liked to tell us was that the next thing Mister Higgerson knew, he was waking up in someplace his eyes had never before seen, and when he reached down to scratch at the place where his right leg used to be, there was no leg there to be scratched, even though, he liked us to know it, it still itched there like there was still a leg there for him to scratch. We told Girl this story, about this leg that was missing, and what Girl wanted to know was, what happened to the leg after it was gone? Which was a thing we did not know, about the leg, and now, it is too late, because not only is Mister Higgerson's leg still gone, now Mister Higgerson himself is gone away from this place, though the nuts and screws that he used to sell are still inside, sitting inside cardboard boxes still sitting on the shelves. But what happened? This is the question that Girl cannot get past. We tell her we don't know. We tell her about our father, him walking out, into the river, that muddy sky. He was gone, but he was still there, like the itch that old Mister Higgerson felt, Brother explains, and I nod my head to say yes, I agree. We boys went out looking for him, our father, but what we found was better than father. Girl wants to know what was better than a father? Do we have to spell it out? we say. We give Girl this look that says, Doy. Give me a stick, Brother says. He takes hold of a branch from a nearby tree and breaks it off. He takes this stick and uses it as a pencil, as a pen, and the earth is a piece of paper that he is writing on. He writes what it was we found, what word it was that was better than finding our father, and the word is girl. The word girl the way it was meant to be spelled: with twelve r's, thirteen u's, and twenty thousand l's at the end of girl, stretching across the earth.

KATHRYN RANTALA

SISTERS

Once there were two sisters. One of them wore her herself outside in, the other, inside out. In all other ways except age they were alike, as much as sisters can be alike, which is both a lot and not at all. The one sister let everything she saw come in. She took everything in from outside. One day she said: Today I am going to learn Greek; and she did. Another day she said: I am going to be a classical pianist. Sometimes she just took things in without comment: she bought a car; she had a baby. She didn't mention everything. Not, for instance, if she didn't think she was going to keep it very long.

The other sister took everything in, too, but could not use it in any practical way. So everything she took in she thought about, then looked for something she could have that seemed like it. She wore herself inside out. Soon she had a room filled with things she'd taken in and taken out again: crackled icons, miniature amphoras; a machine to play the records she bought after hearing beautiful things. Things from watching her sister; things not from her sister, too: a beautifully bound book; a mouse.

Sometimes the sisters tried each other out. That is, they each tried the reverse. It didn't work very well. One would not take care of her things. The other found she could not speak. Each way required its special skills.

Once they tried to be more like the other. At the end of the day they were halfway this, halfway that. Then they were frightened it might take both of them to make one. Then they were afraid there would be no one left to be a sister to. And then they were afraid they would die.

One day one of them did die. The outside in one. She was lying in her bed thinking how she should go about dying, and then she did. The other one could not believe it and stared for a long time without moving or breathing. The doctor looked at the bed and said: she's gone. A minute or two later the inside out one began to breathe suddenly and with a very deep breath. This alarmed the doctor who turned to look at her. But, as nothing further happened, he left.

When she also left the room she was just her. She didn't know exactly what to do. She had taken in something but could not use it in any practical way. And then she was afraid she would die. And then she was afraid she would not.

CHAD McCAIL

ALIEN GENITAL

1999 Series of 6 images
& 6 text panels.
Gouache on paper.
Images: 59 x 63.8 cm.
Text: 22.23 x 25.12 cm.

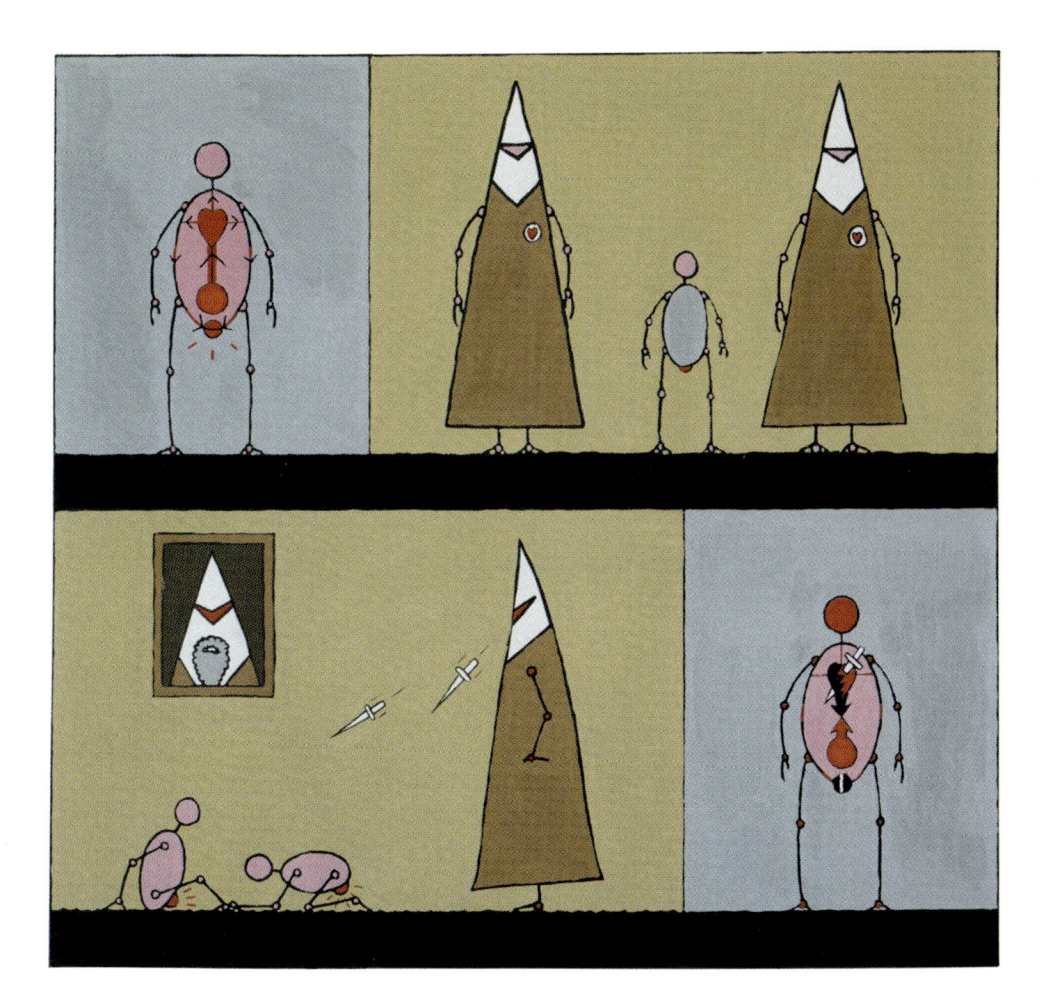

The healthy child has a vital, active genital – the source of life to come. It has two parents. Beneath the portrait of the patriarch, the children explore one another and experience the adult's disapproval. The children receive a profound shock. The source of pleasure is denied and a fundamental and debilitating conflict is established.

The wounded child develops a restricting abdominal ring into which energy is diverted. This ring restricts the flow of energy to the alien genital which is responsible for parental antagonism and painful wounds. At the same time the child retrieves the dagger, symbolic of the adult's antagonism and, adopting the parental role, employs it in play. The parents are not so bothered by this socially licensed activity. However, they are relieved when the child goes to school and as responsibility is transferred, the severe internal condition of teacher and parent is revealed.

The capitalist requires many workers in this condition. He demands them from the politician, who broadcasts the policy. Bureaucrats administrate this policy and the teacher puts it into practice. The child has no choice and is held in place by another restrictive band which it is expected to absorb and internalise.

However, the child rebels. The teacher exercises the authority invested in it and displays a disapproval which the child is able to overcome. With the ban on corporal punishment, the teacher calls in the psychologist who administers a narcotic corrective to the rebellious child.

The child conforms, receiving love for obedience in matching quantities. In this way the child assumes the second restrictive band. The final frame shows the obedient child's self-sacrifice.

The child receives a headset in this state of submission and, with it, the teacher is able to prepare the child for the final stage of its training where it learns the reality of its position in a capitalist democracy. This lesson takes place in a disembodied atmosphere. The child leaves school for the workplace and finally assumes the robe containing the third restrictive band which will mark it as a normal, working adult.

VIRGIL SUÁREZ

A CLOSER LOOK AT THE DETAILS FROM THE ST. PETER ALTARPIECE, ST. PETER MARTYR BY ALONSO BERRUGUETE, 1488–1561

Cloaked in black, this St. Peter is a crow snuck
into the altar, book held open to the "Credo."

A three crowned *palma santa* quill in his right hand,
between book and quill the blade of a knife or sword

coming through his yellow frock, a magenta trickle
like spilled wine. Is this a butcher's knife? Whose?

For the years I lived in Spain and made my parents
take me to see this painting of Berruguete hung

in Museo del Prado because I could not believe
the look in St. Peter Martyr's eyes, fixed complacency

as if to say: *we must all walk wounded, and if you
must walk, you must walk forward to face he who*

plunged the sword into you. But he walks too
with a cleaver whacked into his scalp as if lightning

had struck him twice and he couldn't tell the difference.
Here is a man who doesn't seem too happy or thrilled
to bring you good news that yes, there are people here
in this life all too ready to backstab you, swing an ax

into you as easily as you could shout "Holy scripture!"
Or the way a man will burn with greed because you

walk on, even though you go on wounded but happy.

ROBYN SCHIFF

"JADE CABINET AND ONE LAST THING," ANONYMOUS
hanging scroll
H: 167 cm W: 85 cm
Ming (15th c?)

This is this life. Dawn Gate; the gate is locked. There is the gold of the
    gold pin
in Jade Cabinet's hair and the gold of Gold River. The bridge is wet; the gate
    is locked;
Dawn Gate good morning in which two gold anhingas dry gold wings
    perched upon pins
in Jade Cabinet's hair. Water bird inadequately evolved to swim and fly both
    in the same
hunt, no oil on the wings. Court Goldsmith says *for your daughter* to Jade
    Cabinet's
father.

The gold moon is the sun, it's that early. A night-guard hovers, or is that the
    after life?
A life along side this life unintelligibly played in low lighting. This is this life.
    A crowd
in the foreground gathers in the dark. A crowd to the left disperses.
So these are clouds? Smoke from a faraway fire? Heaven's Honor Guard
forms on the furthest peak of the mountain. No. Flowers in uniform blue.
Perspective is such.

Much closer on a low hill the essence each figure exudes is dust off paper.
Centuries of unrolling have lent an uncertain glow to the painting.
Hesitance is a shade of gold in which Jade Cabinet can't see the night-guard.
This is this life listening for one footstep in the world, one brow cocked to show
she hears one.

IMAGINATION

At Rachel's wedding when the groomsmen hoisted Rachel in a chair above
    our heads
she slid so gracefully off, each satin-covered button skimmed the seat. Tiny
    buttons,
there must have been two dozen up the bodice, each counted in a
    satin-covered ping
against the dinner chair. She hadn't eaten. Nerves and to close the dress.
The wisp of her loosened and came forward like love in a dream lewdly lights
a strange acquaintance whom it has possessed and made seductive.
Lofty thought, into the other imagination, lies down.
And not in dream only; light also resuggests objects on a real life table:
someone comes to breakfast and is no longer beautiful.
It must be the wind that keeps closing the closed door.
I keep thinking someone is coming up the back stairs when I remember
"back stairs" are a romantic construct of a different house in which servants
    no longer even
hurry about discreet quarters hidden beyond the bookcase. It would be a
    good night

if each jolt was justified. It would mean so much
to wake up and know just what is needed. Listening to my neighbor
    practicing guitar
too slowly for the melody to grow familiar, I am with him, but he is alone.

ROBERT COOVER

LUCKY PIERRE THAWS OUT

Focus, fading in, on fallen man fucking. It is understood that this is who he is, what he does, what he must do, it is his karma. He is a man who fucks. His head is still white with melting snow, his poor flesh bluish, his eyes are closed, their lashes frozen shut by frozen tears, but his hips are rising and falling steadily like sluggish gray waves lapping a wintry beach (the only sound to be heard is something like this, or it might be the sound of a thousand people settling into cushioned seats in a moviehouse, repeated over and over in a continuous loop) and his penis has found a warm place and has lost its frosty chill, the first part of him to do so. Near his ice-encrusted mouth is an ear on a bald head, and his cracked lips are trembling as though he might be whispering into it, but if so, what he says (I was having a terrible nightmare, Cassie…!) is inaudible, maybe his vocal cords are still frozen, his faint words more seen than heard: I had slipped and was falling from a great height…! Or perhaps he is falling still, falls now, for his embrace of Cassie's body, more felt than seen, is overlaid by the continuing image of all his women, his co-stars, high up above him in the blowing snow, reaching out for him as he drops away, his frozen hands grasping at that lifeline they've tossed him which is not one. But it is a fading image, much as when a dream ends, overtaken by

Cassie's emerging presence like a slow lap dissolve, and he decides (his eyelashes melt and he peeks out at her delicately whorled ear, sitting on her shaved scalp like a rubber viewfinder cup) that if he is falling still he will accept this present illusion, for it is immensely comforting and cushions the dread of impact and of oblivion.

How did he get here? She found him in the storm, this poor lost film hero, frozen solid on the tenement stoop and she chipped him loose and carried him back to her squat and proceeded to thaw him out with her breath and tongue and with her speaking hands and other healing parts. That, anyway, is how he understands it (the others are far up above him now, almost out of sight and fading, backlit by the beam of light pouring out of the portal wherein they cluster, looking more like one woman than eight or nine, and more like Cassie's ear than either, yes, away they go, can't see them now, gone), and whether that understanding is something he achieves with his own crystallized lobes or is merely provided to him by the script, he surrenders to it and to her holistic therapy, fucking himself (or being fucked, for she has been the initiatrix, he merely her passive acolyte) back to health and sanity, what passes for it in this dying world. I was completely iced up, Cassie, I couldn't feel a thing, he whispers, but though his mouth is open and a frosty cloud emerges, no sound comes out. I felt like the time-lapse man! Even my name had frozen up and fallen off, I was nobody! YOU ARE WHO YOU ARE, she replies, a reply he does not hear but reads, as though she were writing it directly on his forebrain in a black place somewhere behind his eyes.

Earlier—if it is possible to speak of "earlier" around Cassie (if it is possible to speak at all), for whom all time is space, all events simultaneous, all clips interchangeable—

when he complained—though he could not even speak, could not open his mouth, could not breathe, he was nothing but a blue lump of ice in her version of things, his miserable words tracking through his brain like a little train pulling a string of loaded boxcars through a blizzard up a frozen mountainside (My heart is faint within me, he seemed to be wailing—this is a kind of memory emerging more from her body than from his, the words as new to him now as when, presumably, he first issued them—Listen when I groan, there is none to comfort me…)—she told him that he must accept his suffering (the train meanwhile had fallen off its rails), for he was engaged in an intuitive, visionary mode of fucking that was intimately and mysteriously linked to an eternal truth that compelled expression (the battered train was numbly crawling back up the mountainside once more, its mission forgotten, load lost, but chugging away dutifully), no matter how dreadful the consequences. She delivered this message somewhere in the region of his liver for that was, as she called it, THE ORGAN OF PARADOX (though weren't they all?), for by then she was deep into one of her penetrating multisensory rubdowns, bringing him back to life again with her warm oiled fingers and with her juices, mouth, and exhalations.

When she'd first brought him back here, as he was coming to understand it, or to remember it, as if his ponderous thrusts were evoking informative flashbacks, she'd snapped away his frozen clothes like knocking loose plaster off a wall and set him on his knees and forehead, as he was still locked in the sitting position and tended to rock if placed upon his back. He was lifeless and all shrunk up, as white and hard as marble, and not a breath in him, so she chipped the ice out of his anus to create a blowhole and put her mouth to it and sufflated him from there, the first sensation that he had of her. He was still falling then, or supposed he was, and he felt like he was taking wind up his ass from the speed of his fall, though it was a warm wind and it gave him a certain pleasure, even if pleasure was not foremost on his mind at that moment. She tipped him over (he seems to recall the loud knock his frozen body made when it banged upon her barren wooden floor, like a hammer blow, though in the nightmare he was having it was more like an anticipated terror, that bang, than a reality) and sucked the frozen snot out of his nostrils to get his wind machine working from top to bottom, then rolled him onto his back, petrified knees in the air, so that she might work on his heart and testicles, the latter shriveled and hard as little brass worry marbles, but which she labeled THE PLACE WHERE PRIVATE MEANING AND THE DIVINE ORDER MEET. That was also, Cleo once told him, the standard definition of nonsense, and Cassie would not have argued with that, but would have taken it as further encomium. The heart, as furnace and pump room (otherwise vastly overrated, in Cassie's view), needed immediate attention to set that hallowed meeting place thrumming once more, but the capricious brain, mostly obstructive when not pharmaceutically assisted, could wait as it would probably just undermine her therapeutics. She melted the surface frost with her breath, straddled him and rubbed herself about to oil his chest and belly, and then, as he began to thaw, dug in deep with her cunning fingers, pushing her hot body oils in and around the contractile fibrils and the tendons, stroking the dead nerves to restore the current (LET THERE BE LIGHTNING, she seemed to say—though none of these words were actually hers of course, she has no words, they were more like rough translations of the movements of her expressive fingers—LET THERE BE REVELATION AT TWENTYFOUR TIMES A SECOND!), massaging his heart and other involuntary muscles (meaning most of the ones he had), using her own secret gateways through the abdominal wall to reactivate his organs, knead his viscera, cleanse them of what she called, or her fingers did, THE ILLUSION OF PARTICULARS, penetrating ever deeper and delivering her little messages as she moved about.

HE FUCKS IN THE LANGUAGE OF THE WOUND ITSELF, her hands went on as they untied and reknotted his navel, then squeezed in to melt his kidneys with fondlings like sympathetic murmurings, her mouth meanwhile taking in his testicles and rolling them about on the tongue until they softened up and stopped their metallic clacking. Their delivery mechanism, though spiritually of less interest to her, was rigid as always and frozen rock-hard to boot, so she lowered herself over it, careful not to snap it off, shuddering when it entered her like an icicle in a bun-warmer, sizzling and popping. HE DOES NOT EXORCIZE THE PAIN, he seemed to see her vagina say in a message that ran the length of his cold brittle tube, ending somewhere in the region of his Cowper's gland, BUT PROLONGS IT EXCRUCIATINGLY, ENCOURAGING IT TO BREED NEW PAIN, IN HIS DEVOUT EFFORT TO ATTAIN TRANSCENDENCE, TO UNIFY THE WORLD'S MAD SCATTER, TO ACHIEVE EXEMPLARY HARMONY. His awakening scrotum, cozied in the sleek cheeks of her uplifted behind, were emitting their own messages by this time, mostly doleful and skeptical expressions of the bleakest nature, which she sucked up and acknowledged: AN IMPOSSIBLE ENTERPRISE OF COURSE, HE MUST FAIL OVER AND OVER AGAIN, BUT IN HIS FAILURE AND IN HIS PAIN AND DESPAIR HE WILL CREATE BEAUTY, THE ONLY KIND OF BEAUTY IMAGINABLE IN THIS PARTICULATE ABSURDITY WHICH MEN CALL THE UNIVERSE. Perhaps by this time, she had pressed on to the area of his rectum, for he was indeed now feeling a certain creative movement there in its upper regions.

How he got into the missionary position from his inert knees-high rock on the wooden floor under Cassie is not clear to him, but then continuity has never been a notable feature of his career, nor clarity either for that matter, especially in Cassie's enigmatic company; something happens and then something else happens, and all he can do is accept what comes and savor the best of it. And fucking Cassie is about as good as it gets, for it is a pleasurable agitation in an ethereally beautiful vessel, and at the same time an easeful path to inner peace. The solitary one. He has often thought that, if he does have to die (and who's to say, maybe he doesn't—he's been called an "immortal" in all the media, has he not, and when he asked Clara about it, she assured him that, yes, that's virtually so), he would like to die fucking Cassie. The hoarfrost that rimed shut his eyelids has melted, making it seem as if he's crying (perhaps he is), and now, pressing his face against Cassie's smooth bald head to thaw out the rest of it, he can see, projected down inside her inner ear, a live digitized video transmission of his erected cock, no longer ice-blue but buffed to a glistening salmon pink, sliding majestically in and out of her moist hairless crease. This is a very soothing sight. In it goes until pubic bone meets pubic bone like the closing of a gate, cushioned by his nest of hair, her fleshy pillow; then slowly out again until the engorged lip of the crown is glimpsed, stroking the clitoris as a knuckled thumb might flick a marble (this more felt than seen), his ruddy testicles drawn up tight under the rising and falling anus above like an exposed heart worn there openly on his perineum's sleeve as a sign of his humble acquiescence and his gratitude and his tender vulnerability; and then back in again, submerging its full length as though seeking some ultimate connection, not merely with this particular woman, but with the whole of existence, or at least that portion of it as bodied forth between her mysterious thighs. It is, like all of Cassie's poems-in-motion, a work of art that will last forever (though she throws everything away, her tapes and films have to be rescued piecemeal from her bins)—so masterfully simple, so effortless, direct, and aesthetically pure, stripped of all extraneous gesture, in the way that her body has been stripped of all hair and ornament. Yet, for all its self-denying simplicity, it is a work of immense scale and astonishing richness, austere yet gorgeously radiant, a moving image that opens up in him a curious mental space, separate from but linked to that part of his mind (that involuntary muscle is now thawing, too, and going its own way) that takes in the filmed action, wherein he contemplates, as though it were other, his own being. Watching it is like gazing up, while stoned, at a starry night sky, a real one, not a studio mock-up, and it releases him from his earthbound fears and anxieties and from the absurdity of struggle and mad ambition, and makes him feel, as he so rarely feels (in… and out… and in… and out…), at home in the cosmos.

As, mesmerized, he watches, fucks and watches, a second delayed image of his rearing and plunging cock is superimposed upon the first one, following it precisely like a wave lapping another wave, and then a third appears, slightly faster, and a fourth, faster still, and a fifth and a sixth in fugal procession, the patterns changing slightly from image to image, creating an inexhaustible variety of rhythmic structures, and as the overlaid images rub against one another, accompanied by the percussive resonances emerging now from the fleshy collisions, the tempo gradually builds toward a thematic urgency that compels his attention even as that attention is being sucked away with even greater urgency toward his loins. What he sees now in Cassie's ear, though still the same subject, is no longer so precise as a star-studded night sky, but more like scudding clouds rolling in, pink and wet and ceaselessly reshaping themselves in their mounting tumult. This tumult can be heard as well as seen, the reverberant beat of the damp pubic collisions resolving now to massive achromatic chords, riven by the strident noises of the city leaking in like a stuttering melody: whistles, horns, sirens, clattery falls and crashes. All of it proceeds, not by successive rapid contrasts, but by a slow piling up of simultaneous layers, proposing a profusion of expressive possibilities, even while narrowing rapidly to just one. Oh yes, let it come! Her hands are still prowling his insides (AND THEN..., they seem to be saying, or writing, somewhere halfway down his spine) and he can feel her vaginal walls contracting and relaxing now as her own orgasms begin.

Before the storm can break, however, a finger appears and sweeps the clouds aside and pushes into what can now be seen as a soft place between his dancing scrotum and anus as though to locate there an ancient entranceway sealed over by time, and he feels a delicious tension but no release and his prick dips for a moment as though her finger has pressed a switch and the storm subsides and the frantic fugato rhythms slow to a steady rise and fall and the fleshy elements return in all their clarity and radiance, and then he's ready to go again. Everything is more liquid now and more aromatic (yes, he can smell again! she is restoring him in all his parts!) and he is gripped at the root by powerful pulsing contractions more felt than seen or heard, yet echoed in plangent cadences rising up as if from the earth below. Cassie, through austere self-discipline and purity of heart and will, has moved beyond multiple orgasms into prolonged compound orgasms, which she has been known to hold for hours, maybe even days (never sure about time around Cassie—even now, her slippery fingers pushing down into the base of his spine seem to be announcing: THE NEXT DAY...), and though he must always fail her (she casts no blame, in her universal love she is beyond censure and reward) and is driven more to anxiety than to delight by the effort demanded, he does all that he can to stay with her as long as possible and willingly accepts whatever she does in her wisdom to help him, for he knows that fucking Cassie to the edge of her own rapture is the closest he will ever come to experiencing—if only vicariously—nirvana.

Just before it is too late—he feels like his whole body is an erogenous zone, erect and awash in Cassie's magical juices—her finger reappears and plugs once more the collapsing dike within, and does so repeatedly, and so the rhythm of tension and the temporary subsidence of tension builds, gathering in momentum and complexity, the monumental image of pounding cock and cunt (he is not even looking into her ear any longer, but he can still see the projected image as if it were sitting between his eyes on the bridge of his nose) absorbing into itself fleeting hints of montaged visual elements both cosmic and human and acquiring thereby textures of luminous clarity and teeming inner life, taking him to the brink again and again, and he decides at last—A WEEK LATER... is the message tickling the rim of his anus—or his gonads decide for him, his entire focus now surging toward the end of his throbbing organ, that this—oh wow!—is as close as he'll try to get on this occasion to Cassie's peak, he's (there's a tremendous pressure in his head and in his chest and he can hear a fast approaching climax of whooping horns) ready to blow. But Cassie's film no longer coincides precisely with his felt experience, for he believes himself still to be plunging away from above, while the bodies in the film seem to be slowly rolling across the wooden floor, or else the room is rolling around the bodies, the floor appearing and disappearing between the knotted cheeks of Cassie's flawless ass, displaced as it vanishes with views of the barren white room—wall, ceiling, wall, floor, wall, ceiling, wall—and these views in turn are displaced by glimpses of other rooms and other spaces, interior and exterior, her vagina meanwhile tightening, her serial orgasms closer and closer together like a vibrating electrical current. Faster and faster the room whirls around them, dizzying him with its gathering speed, the floor cracking his ass with each revolution like a wooden paddle—Wait a minute, Cassie, he cries, or thinks he cries, I don't feel so good! Let me off for a minute! But the room continues to wheel madly around them, if it still is the room (all he can see now are colors whipping past and growing ever more vibrant—all of this appears between her convulsive cheeks on the screen, but if he should open his eyes—he can't!—he's sure he'd still see the same old wooden floor below him, he's pretty sure), her spasms now more like an oscillating hum, rising in pitch. He would desperately like to come—YEARS PASS is the message quivering at the tip of his penis—but it's not to be. The thumping rotation of the room slows gradually and comes finally to a stop and he finds himself—with a spinning head, aching goolies, and a maddeningly buzzing prick—lying flat out on the floor on his back, all alone, as if, from some great height, he'd fallen here.

KEVIN SAMPSELL

FLYING HORSES

I got off of my horse and watched the burning body. A fireman approached me with a cup of hot coffee. He gave me a photograph of a naked boy with a large sexual organ. I stuck it in my mouth. He sipped his coffee loudly without looking at me and then excused himself to disconnect a hose. I picked up a five dollar bill that he seemed to have dropped on purpose and stuffed it down my pants. Something dripped from my mouth.

A well-dressed man came up to me and asked about my dark glasses. I rubbed the top of my head and made my hair stick up, imitating the flames. The real flames were being fought by fire fighters. They were coming out of an old lady's mouth. Her teeth popped loudly. I got the feeling the fire fighters weren't trying very hard to stop it.

The man who was talking to me tore off my glasses and ran toward the burning lady. I stood frozen, half asleep, half in shock. He threw the glasses at the flaming body like someone pitching a ball in cricket. The body looked lifeless, sort of like a statue. The man then picked up the glasses and tried putting them on the woman's face, but he had a hard time getting around the flames. The fireman who had given me the photograph then tackled the man roughly.

Moments later, a pizza delivery man arrived on the scene to feed everyone. The fire had spread to four or five nearby houses. I found a bench to sit on. A female fire fighter sat next to me and started talking.

"Your Heaven looks just like my Hell," she said.

"What?" I said.

She gave me a sad look, took a bite of pizza, and with her mouth full, began to tell me about Pac-Ten colleges. I watched the burning lady collapse and listened to the female fire fighter. About ten minutes later I noticed we had somehow gotten closer to the still-burning body. I turned around and discovered the man who had taken my glasses was slowly and quietly pushing our bench closer to the flames.

"You stupid little monkey," the female fire fighter said to him.

"Why don't you just go home and adjust the insurance policies like you're supposed to?"

The man clenched his fists and fidgeted with his facial expressions, like he was trying to decide if he should hit her or not. I got in between them and offered the man five dollars to go away. He raised it to six and we settled. All of a sudden he looked at ease and even extended his hand to shake. Before getting into his car he stood with the driver door open, laughing repulsively until the fireman threatened to tackle him again.

"You're a one-eyed fool," the female fire fighter said to me.

The rest of the fire fighters were struggling with several powerful hoses while eating pizza at the same time. The water was spraying frantically into houses that weren't even on fire.

I was getting ready to ride my horse back home when I noticed the old lady who had been on fire was standing up and brushing ashes off of her tattered clothes. She seemed to be fine. I almost wanted to help her but felt embarrassed about the cowboy suit I was wearing. She looked nervously at the clumsy fire fighters as she crouched behind a car, andthen ran into one of the burning houses without anyone seeing.

    I walked over to my horse and untied the rope. I patted her muscular neck and brushed the rough patches of hair on her side. Her silhouette looked awesome in the firelight. I whispered into her ear and let her run home by herself. I felt good despite my blurry vision.

CHRISTOPHER KENNEDY

DECOMPOSITION #249

The elephant trundled with its legs in muck, while the airplane flew across the sky. For once the baker and the loaf of bread walked hand in hand down Main Street unashamed of their love, one eventually devouring the other. The night air tasted like a dill pickle.

Behind the bowling alley, kids were drinking wine with Christ. Later, a cop handcuffed himself to his mother as his crime waved in the wind like a worn flag. At last the man in the hearse woke up from his bad dream—the birth of a child that looked like him.

Suddenly all birds fell out of their trees. Only one more Sunday and this life will be over. *Oh calendar, refrain from your daily torture*, the elephant trumpeted, then disappeared.

TRIVIA

There were two dogs running the ditch next to a country road. A car drove past and veered out of control. It struck a tree, a large sugar maple, the state tree of New York, and burst into flames. Did I say two dogs? There were three, one of them a rare breed.

THE BROKEN LOCK

The family sat down to dinner. The mother led them in saying grace. *...and to my oldest son, I say, I eat the dust of your leaving.* Then, the uncomfortable silence. After dinner, their separate rooms were on fire of a different sort. There were only two of them. A mother and a son. All night, the wind spread the flames, but no one noticed, or if they did, no one cared to call out. Though, in their defense, fire is often invisible, a pale blue flame and a crackling sound like a broken lock on an empty gun cabinet.

NORMAN LOCK

OPERA WITH MOON SNAILS
for Meredith Lock

He had caused Algiers to appear in the opera house, a little of it, the part of it inside the old city walls, the Kasbah, Joseph Cornell had caused it, we did not know how and marveled, a thin music wound like adders through the crooked streets, we loved the red fezzes, the Arab women, the spiced and orangey air, the boat from Marseilles bumped against the dock and sighed, Méliès arrived to make a film of the Kasbah, because of the scarcity of dreams, he said unwinding his watch, Berta Kukelvan—the actress—was with him, her wrist in plaster, they had just finished *Le Voyage dans la lune*, the cardboard rocketship stood in a corner of the opera next to a section of the lunar precipice, it is all of it a dream, said Méliès, happily, Joseph Cornell murmured his assent and hung paper lanterns, we watched nervously as he climbed the slender ladder into the darkness, the moon next if you please, requested Méliès adjusting his Kinétograph lens, the moon, alas, is torn! the impresario replied, the rocket had struck it and Berta Kukelvan had tumbled out injuring her wrist on a picnic hamper, thus the plaster cast which had made us wonder in secret, she disappeared now into the depths of the Kasbah in order to, as she said, immerse herself in her role, we wished her *bon chance*! waving our programs encouragingly, the sun fell behind the rocky hills of Africa, we were afraid of the strangeness of it all, what shall we do until the light comes again? we asked ourselves, the ocean that slid back and forth between Algeria and Spain rattled over stones, hissed in retreat from the beach, roared down the black jetties, we smoked to make a little light in the night, it was then Méliès turning his camera towards the shore cried out to us—look! *look*, my friends! he cranked his camera ecstatically, the beach! the beach shone with moon snails blue and coolly lunar, an unexplainable stage effect provided by Joseph Cornell for his opera of the Kasbah, for which Méliès thanked him, as we too do thank him for this dream.

THE OPERA OF THE DROWNED

Not all of those who were there were famous, but one was, Verne was certainly, Jules Verne was although he was dead, at the time *The Opera of the Drowned* was being performed Jules Verne was quite happily dead, but that did not stop him from coming to see the production which was brilliant, many said, I agree and so does Anne and George does too, Wallace, however, disagrees, to this day Wallace says this particular opera is abysmal, a waste of the composer's feeble ability, his slim talent, but one thing is certain and ungainsayable for me: Jules Verne did come to see it, *The Opera of the Drowned*, came and sat in the box reserved for the most famous, even the dead most famous, and I could not take my eyes from him looking at him through the opera glass that was a *vade mecum* of my life at that time, I was seeing so many operas at that time of my life with Anne, with George, not with Wallace if I could help it for he is not sympathetic, not in the way George and Anne are, all of us except Wallace looked at Jules Verne in his rococo box and could not help wonder what he was making of it, this opera that had as its *mise en scène* a submarine, of course this was what had persuaded Jules Verne to leave his quiet fame, his ungainsayable importance as a precursor to science fiction, a past practitioner of fantastic literature all of us except Wallace admire, I later asked him, Jules Verne, as both he and I happened together to present our checks to the pretty hat check girl and together receive our hats so uncannily alike, in fact, there was a little comic confusion with the hats of the kind so dear to vaudevillians, what do you think of the opera, M. Verne? he answered me in his language, which is or was of course French, something incomprehensible to me having not the language, but whatever he said, whatever the gist, his having said it proved ungainsayably that this Jules Verne was not a cardboard prop or mannequin as Wallace claimed, propped up in the box reserved for the illustrious as part of the opera production, no, not at all I said to George and Anne and Wallace later in the hotel barroom, Wallace, however, could not be shaken from his unattractive cynicism, he claimed it was not Jules Verne but an impersonator hired by the management to gull the gullible, I detest Wallace and told him so then even if he had taken as his motto the same one J. J. Rousseau had from Juvenal, his *Satires*: *vitam impendere vero*: to consecrate life to truth, even so I tell you Wallace is a liar and no friend to opera where to be gulled is a pleasure, the greatest possible pleasure, and artifice is why we go to see opera, isn't it?

THE OPERA OF DESIRE

Hubble came with a telescope, with which to view the most distant skies, he said, the skies, however, were obscured by a palpable darkness at the top of the opera house, above the farthest platforms where the trapeze artists loitered unseen by us but apparent to our imaginations, we liked his tweed knickers and told him so, they become you! we shouted, for his attention was on the instrument, he was smitten! what he had seen in the eyepiece beguiled him completely and brought him to the edge of a swoon, it was Lola Montes, she who had been the lover of Franz Liszt and also of King Ludwig of Bavaria whom the world called Mad, she now became the object of Edwin Hubble's desire, she is delicious! he said in an aside overheard by the impresario as he smoked a cigarette with the handsome young tenor waiting to make his entrance into Jules Massenet's opera *Werther*, it is all, the impresario said, about desire, Werther bit his hand, yes! he cried anguished, yes! desire is a force akin to gravitation, the impresario continued, it is it that causes the stars to chase each other forever outward, the stars in their red shifts, he knows, Edwin knows, and so did Liszt and the King of Bavaria, and once even I, the impresario, knew, but—the tenor reminded him—Liszt died young and Mad Ludwig drowned himself in the Starnberger and Lola Montes became a circus exhibit, but ah! the impresario answered, they flew, you know, until the end they all of them defied gravity such was the strength of their desire—who, we wondered, who then is Hubble peering at through his telescope, Lola Montes having long ago died? from his opera box Joseph Cornell said: her remnant of light still desiring.

CORMAC JAMES

THE DISAPPEARANCE OF MISS EFFIE SKINNER

Lately, my father has been trying to show an interest in what I do, or at least to find some common ground between us. On his side he has great faith in local history. Since he stopped drinking, that's become his vice. For him, however, history seems to be something peculiar to the past. Or maybe it would be more accurate to say that its significance seems to lie in its remoteness from his own life. So, the past he has unearthed is a sequence of murders, betrayals, sinister affinities or coincidences, and so on—made even more remote by the fact that these things occurred locally, in houses he himself has been in, along paths he himself has trod. I don't say anything about any of this. I try to keep out of it. But he doesn't seem to have heard my silence, and lately, whenever he comes across anything remotely macabre or quirky, he's on the phone to me in a shot, very amiably, as though it's a habit that's been built up over the years. Most recently, he's been going on about this one particular story he thinks I should write about. It concerns a death—possibly a murder— that took place more than a century ago, in Dripsey, a rural district near to where I grew up. All this really came to a head a few days ago, when I returned to his house—my childhood home—for the first time in several years. I've come back to stand for him at his wedding—a nice job for a son.

Up in my old room, I wasn't even finished unpacking when he appeared in the doorway with a big box-file, which he threw onto the bed without a word. I watched it bounce. Just by the sheer size of it, I knew it must have taken him months to compile, maybe longer. It contains anything he considers might be even remotely relevant to the matter in question. What method or criteria he used in the compilation I don't know. Even though I still had to come up with my after-dinner speech, and had more or less set that evening aside to cobble something together—even so, to keep the old man happy I took a look through the file. Besides, it allowed me to forget for a while the duty I'd accepted. I had to say yes or no, and yes seemed the lesser evil.

Here are the basic facts of the case as I see it, with a bit of background first:

Bringing his own troop of horse, a man called Cross came to Ireland with Cromwell's army in 1649. (My father obviously didn't see the need to dig any deeper than that.) Like many other soldiers, after the war (so-called) this man was granted a portion of the conquered territory—in Dripsey, in the county of Cork.[1] His grandson Epinetus—who later also came by land in the county—became a Justice of the Peace in Cork City in 1680, but was not survived by any son of his own. My father, never one to be bettered by that kind of obstacle, has traced the pedigree of Epinetus' brother to one Philip Henry Eustace Cross,[2] born in the family home, "Shandy Hall,"[3] Dripsey, in 1834.

The file includes—from diverse sources—various accounts of this Philip Cross which my father has circled with his trademark orange pencil, as being illustrative of the man's character. An article by a historian named H.W. Gillman, for instance, has a footnote recounting a story about him, which I give here unabridged:

---

[1] *Book of Survey and Distribution of the Kingdom of Ireland*, (1661) p.163.

[2] Or, rather, traced it from Philip Cross backwards.

[3] Not, unfortunately, the house Sterne named his own after—that was up in the north of the county. The IRA burned that one down in the War of Independence.

A gate near the entrance to the deerpark of Shandy Hall still bears the name of Geata-na-Sciursachta, which is Irish-English[4] for 'the scourging gate'. This seems to have been used for the benefit of trespassers on the land. And thereof a story is told; once upon a time a servant of Crowdy of Cloghroe[5] came to the place with a mare on business, for as will be presently noted the Cloghroe folk fostered the breeding of good horses. Crowdy's man trespassed in some unauthorized way on the deerpark, and was promptly tied up and received an allotted number of lashes. His master, to whom he reported the tale on his return home, did not relish this treatment of his servant, and the next day, dressing himself in the latter's clothes, he presented himself with the same mare again to the then Cross of Shandy Hall. Cross bade him go away, but Crowdy said Cross should be off first, and so on; and soon a stiff, honest fight with fists ensued, and Crowdy, who was a powerful man, scored heavily over his antagonist. It is said that Geata-na-Sciursachta fell somewhat into disuse after this episode in its history.[6]

4
There is no such language.

5
A district near to Dripsey.

6
Journal of the Cork Historical and Archaeological Society, (1905), pp.225-6.

The records of the Cork Winter Assizes report that on 27-9-1896, Philip Cross, a magistrate of the county of Cork, was tried at the Quarter Sessions Court for the false imprisonment of one Cormack McCarthy, and, being found guilty was sentenced to imprisonment for one calendar month, and fined £10. In sentencing him, the judge describes the defendant as

> an eccentric, litigious and dominating squireen who seems to derive more pleasure from browbeating his tenants than from combining with them to increase the property's viability.

In August of the next year, in a case brought against him by his brother-in-law, he was up before the courts again for having diverted a stream. In amongst everything else, I came across this information:

> An incident in 1892 when he seized the chattels of an impoverished widowed tenant to compensate for rent unpaid completely alienated him with [sic] his neighbours. Following that his family was boycotted and the Hussars of Blarney fearing the wrath of the farmers, forbad him to hunt with them.[7]

Whatever social life he and his family had must have been hugely reduced after that.

Cross had served "with credit" in the Crimea, in India and in Canada, rising to the rank of Surgeon-Major in the course of twenty years' service. Visiting London in 1879, he met one Laura Mary Marriott, sixteen years his younger; after a courtship that was very short by the standards of the day, they were married. On his retirement, they returned to his family estate, a stud farm, where he lived on his pension and her inheritance, occupying himself in fishing, hunting and shooting on the surrounding countryside.[8] After seven or eight years of marriage, Cross became involved with their children's governess, Miss Euphemia Skinner. Eventually, one evening, on who knows what information, Mrs. Cross insisted to her husband that the young woman be dismissed from her post. After a turbulent night, Cross drove Miss Skinner to Euston (then Kingsbridge) station in Cork, and put her on the mail train to Dublin. Under who knows what—if any—pretence, within a week he himself traveled to Dublin. In a hotel there, he and Miss Skinner shared a room for several nights, signing themselves *Mr. and Mrs. Osborne.* Cross

---

[7] Henchion's *Cork Centenary Remembrancer,* (1992), p.174.

[8] I have a friend who lives out that direction, who even today shoots and fishes on the same lands, although the fishing isn't up to much these days on account of pollution. He recently bought a gun-dog called "*Trigger,*" a name neither of us could take seriously, so I suggested he rechristen her "*Lia,*" Gaelic for "grey," which she is, which he did.

returned to Shandy Hall to hear that his wife had fallen ill on the very day of his departure. Several days passed. To neighbours who inquired about his wife's illness, Cross described its symptoms as "trivial." Nevertheless, after a week, he asked one Dr. Godfrey, a friend, to take a second look at her. In a note in the file, in his own inimitable way, my father writes that this man

> had not been told the full symptoms by Dr. Cross, thought that Laura was suffering from a bilious attack, and he could see no symptoms of Thypoid [sic] Fever. He reassured his friend that nothing more than a strong purge was called for.

She died on the 2nd of June, 1898, and was buried in the local Protestant cemetery two days later.[9] One James Cross, a close relative and an undertaker, took care of the funeral arrangements. To me, there was as yet nothing extraordinary in any of this.

In the following week, Cross visited the cemetery very early each morning—"*to check if the grave had been interfered with,*" my father writes, though I've yet to find this confession in any of the papers included in his file. Cross told one inquiring neighbor that his wife had died of an attack of *angina pectoris*, another that she had died of typhoid, and so on. A fortnight later, he journeyed to London, where he and Miss Skinner were soon married, before returning together to Shandy Hall.

By all accounts it might have been a happy ending for the remaining parties. But someone had prompted Laura Cross to recognize her husband's infidelity, and the same voices now surfaced again, this time whispering to the local constabulary. The body was exhumed, and the autopsy,

[9] The family vault, in the city cathedral, was full.

finding traces of arsenic in the viscera, declared "death by poisoning." Philip Cross was tried between the 14th and the 18th of December, in Cork, and hanged there on the 7th of January, 1899. His last will and testament entrusted his two daughters, "*being of weak intellect,*" to the special care of his brother. His son by his second wife, not yet baptized, was to be named John. Provision was made for the settlement of all outstanding fines and debts. Miss Skinner was bequeathed £60 per annum from the income of his estate. There is no further account of her.[10]

Those are the bones of the story. However, my father would never forgive me if I didn't flesh it out with a few particulars. What he calls "the intimacies of the thing." "*Intimacies.*" Whenever he says this word—which he does at every opportunity, till it's all but empty of meaning—he says it slowly, lasciviously, relishing the sound, the taste of it. "It's been dead long enough," he says. "Breathe some *life* into it." I make no comment, knowing that even expressed indifference, once expressed, would involve me irredeemably in the matter. So I make no comment, and try not to imagine what he thinks I think.

Of course, there are any number of details to choose from in the file. For instance, a few months before her death Mrs. Cross took a long holiday in Scotland, as if she could escape or relieve the isolation she felt in her large country house, amidst a rainswept countryside, hostile tenants, and—to use my father's words—"*totally alienated from her neighbours.*" In letters home to the new governess, she complains of repeated fainting fits and dizziness. The governess assured her it was the foreign air. But Mrs. Cross' return to Shandy Hall found her preoccupied with a fear of death by heart failure. In the month leading up to her death she was constantly vomiting, had diarrhea, and so on,

10
In even the quickest survey of all my father has amassed, one has glimpses of entirely distinct worlds, just as worthy as interest, even by my father's criteria, and of which Cross' world might easily have been the tangent. Eleven days after the execution, for instance, a niece of his was charged with her own husband's death, "*resulting from starvation, from want of proper medical attendance and from neglect.*" This man's sister had several years before bequeathed her entire property—inherited in place of her brother because of their parents' disapproval of his marriage—to this same woman, her brother's wife, Cross' niece, the accused, the bequest being made on the condition that he (the sister's brother, the dead man) be supplied from it "*with farming stock support, sustenance and comfort, such as she herself had*"—in other words, precisely those conditions the accused afterwards failed to meet. (In the end,

recovering from this illness for only a few days, to take one last walk in the wooded hills which stood between her house and the river. I myself have often walked those woods.

The new governess kept a diary, in which a very selective account of this last month is found. For example:

> *26th May:* The rector called. [...] When leaving the rector remarked, in private, upon how inflamed the mistress's eyes showed themselves to be. It is true that she has great difficulty reading. It is left to my hands to write each and every letter for her.
> *30th May:* The rector came to call. Dr. Cross forbad him entry to the house.
> *1st June:* These last three days, the mistress is unable to eat [...] with no more than a cup of milk by her bed.

On the night of the first of June, the servants heard a sudden series of screams from Mrs. Cross' chamber. Everybody froze, wherever they were in the house, whatever they were doing—the housemaid locking up the shutters, the governess reading to the children, the butler in the kitchen, lifting a glass to his lips. They all waited in silence, but no other sound came down to them. Only the two young daughters, it appears, failed to understand what this meant. In a journal to which my father also submits, yet another local historian, Anthony Greene, describes the preparations that followed:

> After making the announcement, Dr. Cross returned upstairs and, with the assistance of a young maid, washed the body clean and laid it out. They dressed Mrs. Cross in a white vest, a nightdress, blue stockings and a band around her head, to keep her mouth closed.[11]

---

the Justice advised the jury that though the woman's conduct might be morally blameworthy, this was a different thing from it being legally criminal.)

11
Anthony Greene, "Reasonable Doubt: The Trial and Execution of Dr. Philip Cross." *The Coachford Record*, Vol 1, p.43.

12
It was intended to store them here until the trial, but they were soon transferred—with the rest of the proceedings—to Burke's Hotel, the ballroom of which would facilitate the enormous interest of the public.

13
The coroner.

14
Ibid., pp.49-50.

15
In the course of which three buttons were torn from the inspector's tunic, and damage done to a bystander's perambulator, for the cost of the replacement of which Cross would later be fined.

After the (clandestine) exhumation, the remains were brought to Cork, to the city courthouse.[12] Greene insists on giving us the details:

> Meanwhile Dr. Pearson[13] removed parts of the body, which he took to Cork City for analysis. The body was then returned to the graveyard in a donkey cart and re-interred. On the following day Dr. Pearson returned, re-exhumed the unfortunate body and removed further samples [...] using Marsh's test, then relatively new, [he] established the presence of arsenic in the body. These findings were conveyed to the police.[14]

On the day following the second exhumation, on the platform of Kingsbridge station, Philip Cross was approached by three constables and an inspector. After a scuffle,[15] he was taken into custody, where he was charged with the willful murder of his first wife.[16]

Cross appeared in court wearing a green tweed suit with matching scarf. He was otherwise described by one reporter as

> no ordinary man. With his upright, martial bearing and well-cut features, he has often, while following the hounds, evoked general admiration from his neighbours [...] It was remarked that the prisoner's beard was noticeably more grey than hitherto.[17]

The prosecution's case goes over most of what I've related so far—the affair, etc., adding only several "expert" testimonies, concerning typhoid, toxins, Mrs. Cross' health, and so on.[18] The servants testified to having supplied their mistress with a diet of macaroni, cornflower, and sago,

---

16 Cross at once applied to the Queen's Bench (The High Court) to have his trial transferred to Dublin, on the grounds that a fair hearing would be impossible in Cork, because of various rumors then in circulation, his unpopularity, and the "*heightened feelings caused by press reports.*" The trial was duly transferred, but immediately moved back when the prosecutor swore that no prejudicial rumors were currently circulating in the city. Greene describes this declaration as "incredible," and goes on to describe the trial as "a media sensation," for which "*applications for tickets were received from some 5,000 people, including we are told 'ladies of quality!'.*" The exclamation mark, I imagine, is in fact his own.

17 *The Cork Evening Examiner*, 15-12-1898, p.2.

18 One such testimony came from a friend of the deceased,

declaring that she was "addicted" to this last substance.[19] They also confessed to having seen Dr. Cross give his wife chlorodyne[20] on many occasions, and to having seen a bottle of white powder amongst the sundries on her vanity table. Despite extensive questioning, they were unable to conceive what this white powder might have been. A hotel manager was summoned from Dublin to give evidence, with his receptionist. Yes, they did think it strange that a man whose bags were marked "P. X." would sign himself "Mr. Osborne." One Denis Griffin, Sub-Postmaster at Dripsey, gave evidence of the contents of various correspondences between Dr. Cross and Miss Skinner. On cross-examination,[21] the coroner admitted to:

1. Having placed more than one of the organs examined in the same dish.
2. Having never previously performed Marsh's Test, nor—in the case at hand—having tested for two other substances which also produce positive results to said test.
3. Having never previously investigated a case of arsenic poisoning.
4. Having never previously examined an alleged murder victim.
5. Having carried out the necropsy without assistance.
6. Having neglected to retain the samples.

My father's judgement on the witnesses, en bloc: "[they] *proved nothing but the weakness of their own intellect.*" Nor did the tone of the prosecutor's speech add much to the proceedings; with a disingenuous sentimentality, for instance, he insists on referring to the prisoner's wife as "*the mother of his innocent children,*" and at one point describes the alleged crime as

---

whose expertise consisted in having discussed poisons with a brother-in-law several years previously, and once read a book on the subject. It was this witness who "*saw Dr. Cross give his wife a bowl of chicken broth on one occasion.*"

19
A form of starch.

20
A mild form of analgesic.

21
My father makes much of the pun.

one of the most horrible that has ever disgraced our common humanity [...] in order that its author might gratify his lust for the young woman he had seduced.[22]

The defense called only one witness[23]—Henrietta Cross, a sister of the accused. She told of having discussed, both with the deceased and with her own dentist, the use of arsenic for certain cosmetic purposes,[24] and of having obtained from a "respectable" chemist in the city several prescriptions of it for the deceased "*on word of such express purpose.*" The Justice,[25] however, believing Miss Cross to be doing all in her power to serve his brother's interests before those of justice, invited her to leave the stand. Her evidence was struck from the books, and the jurymen instructed to strike it from their memories.

The Justice summed up the case before sending the jury out, his speech being reported in full in the press. He repeatedly reminds them that the only substantive charge Philip Cross faces is that of murder. Illicit relations, while undoubtedly reprehensible, remained the concern of a higher judge, Whose role they should not presume to usurp. Nevertheless, he deals at length with the "improper conduct" of the accused, and on such traits of character as might be inferred from it. He also instructs:

> Let them put arsenic for the complexion out of the question—the idea of a lady eighteen years married and her two daughters using arsenic!

The judge also recapitulates, in part, various testimonies heard by the court—reminding the jury, for instance, that the prisoner's announcement of his wife's death to the staff was

---

22 In his trademark orange pencil, my father has put a question mark over "he."

23 Prior to The Criminal Evidence Act of 1900, "*An accused person may not give evidence at his* [sic] *own trial.*"

24 At that time arsenic was sometimes used to whiten the skin.

25 Possessing, for the time, the peculiarly Irish name of Murphy.

26 There is no orange pencil under this line.

27 The coroner.

28 Greene, pp.57-8. This same Dr. C.Y. Pearson later wrote an article entitled "The Medico-legal Aspects of the Case of Philip Cross" (*Journal of the Medical Profession of Ireland*, Spring, 1899, pp.25-41, and simultaneously extracted in the press), in an attempt both to vindicate himself and to leave "*a permanent record*

"*without any sign of natural feeling on his part, no wailing or expression of grief.*"[26]

Greene's own account of what happened next is better than any wording I could ever contrive:

> It suddenly occurred to the learned Judge that the body had never been identified and a Dr. Crowley was called for this purpose, which he did. The jury was then sent out. The jury reappeared twice, first to ask Dr. Pearson[27] if he would swear on the Bible that Mrs. Cross had died of arsenic poisoning, which he did at the judge's request, and the second time to ask for a photograph of Miss Skinner. This was provided. Several minutes later they returned and delivered a verdict of GUILTY.[28]

I cannot understand why Cross accepted the traditional opportunity to speak before sentence was pronounced. His speech is a collection of clichés at once familiar and contradictory,[29] as if Cross has finally accepted his role, and the lines that go with it: he protests his complete innocence, of course, refers to injustice in general, the miscarriage of justice in particular, and finally asks if it is likely that a man of his age would risk so much for such a "slip" of a girl. Why speak, if this is what comes out? Is he afraid that the silence of every man in the dock is the same—that history might burden him with a silence not his own? Is that why he contrives his own silence, these other men's words, being in his mind the lesser of two evils? Even so, being taken from the court, he was hissed, booed, and spat upon by his audience.

Philip Cross' appeal to the Queen's proxy, the Irish Lord Lieutenant, was denied, and a gentleman from Peterborough, one Mr. Berry, was sent for to perform his 113th execution.

One local newspaper advertised and published a series

---

for future readers who can have no other means of becoming acquainted with the true facts and history of the case." Its essential point is that any member of Cross' profession could easily have obtained a poison not traceable in the body. (Yet he later praises Cross' "choice" of poison, it being "*without odour, taste, or colour—therefore most easy of administration.*") Elsewhere in this article, Pearson ridicules the likening, by the defense attorney, of the liver to a sponge—the attorney attempting to prove that the organ could not possibly have "soaked up" as much arsenic as the coroner testified it had. Pearson believes that the inaccuracy of this "metaphor" "*goes to show the utter absurdity of anyone trying to deal with scientific matters on [sic] which they are wholly ignorant.*"

29
In the same way that my own father, say, will proclaim: "Not by whom, but how!" when it suits him, only to muse ten minutes later that "An eagle doth not generate pigeons…"

of articles and "letters to the editor," generally in support of the outcome of the case, and also printed accounts of:

1. Dr. Philip Cross' defiant attitude.
2. Dr. Philip Cross' "*sang froid.*"
3. Dr. Philip Cross' heartless refusal to allow his children or wife to visit him.
4. Dr. Philip Cross' complaints about prison food.

It also reported the rumor that Cross had confessed at the last minute. A rival paper, however, claims that the prisoner maintained his innocence to the end, reporting that while the chaplain visited Cross regularly in the three weeks between sentence and execution, he was always met with a "*polite but firm*" refusal of his ministrations.

All applications of the press to be present at "the event" were refused, leading one editorial to complain that the authorities had "*acted very improperly in thus declining to gratify the natural curiosity of the public.*"[30] Nevertheless, full accounts of "the event" appeared in this same paper the very same day, describing what the prisoner wore, how he walked, and how

> When the rope had been adjusted, he turned to the chaplain, as if desirous of uttering a few words to him. But, before he could frame a sentence, the trap on which he stood fell apart beneath his feet, and, the next moment, Philip Cross was launched into eternity.[31]

In a local tavern, one reporter overhears Mr. Berry[32] describe the prisoner passing away "*as peaceful as a summer eve.*"[33]

The execution, however, did not return the matter to the private domain. Indeed, it could be said that the press

---

[30] *The Cork Evening Examiner*, 12-1-1899, p.2.

[31] Ibid., p.12.

[32] Of whom the following portrait is given in an adjacent article: "*In his private capacity, Mr. Beery* [sic] *does a considerable business in selling bacon on commission. He is also an ardent pigeon fancier, and, in his leisure hours, he is a keen disciple of Izaac Walton.*"

[33] The autopsy of the executed, which could not take place without the presence of this same executioner, is of interest only insofar as it mentions several "decorations" found on the remains, one of which is playfully described as consisting of "*a pack of hounds tattooed down the back, with the fox going to earth in the appropriate place.*" Cross was buried in prison grounds.

fuelled as much as reflected the public debate regarding the circumstances of the alleged crime. With so many publications competing for sensational material, one even went so far as to print lengthy extracts from the statement submitted by the coroner[34] to the press in the hope of dispelling certain myths already gaining currency. From those extracts I include these:

> No external marks of violence were discernible on the victim's body. A rigorous internal examination showed the absence of any evidence of violence to the larynx, trachea, vagina, anus or rectum, or inner surfaces or borders of the mouth [...] The only evidences of putrefaction present in the abdomen were found in the liver; the gall-bladder contained a small amount of bile; the spleen and kidneys were healthy; the bladder was empty; the uterus and ovaries too presented a healthy appearance.

In support of various claims made in this same release, Dr. Pearson variously refers to his own testimony,[35] concluding:

> he [Cross] exhibited it [the arsenic] in repeated doses, so as to produce a prolonged illness, and gave chlorodyne to mask the painful symptoms; in so doing, he also prepared her [Mrs. Cross] relatives and friends for her inevitable, approaching death.

What the speculations of the day were in light of all this, there is no way of knowing. Time has put them beyond reach. But a hundred years on, this particular aspect of the case prompts Greene to propose:

---

34 Cf. fn. 31.

35 Where, for example, he states that the administration of a narcotic would have the effect of diminishing or preventing the painful symptoms which arsenic might cause, and how one such narcotic—chlorodyne—was on record as having been frequently ingested by Mrs. Cross.

Owing to the fact that repeated doses must have been administered in order to produce the symptoms present in this case, the possibility of accidental administration cannot be admitted, whereas if it was put forward that Laura, with the object of taking her own life, deliberately took the poisons herself on repeated occasions, I should be led to believe that she subjected herself to a slow and painful form of lingering torture such as is rarely to be found recorded in all of toxicological literature.[36]

He insists:

Despite the good judge's disbelief, arsenic was commonly used for the complexion, and we know that Mrs. Cross did indeed discuss its use for that purpose. Despite the good judge's disbelief[37] arsenic was used for stomach upsets and "feminine complaints"—Milner's Medical Dictionary, a common text book at the time, makes several references to its use.[38]

Consequently, he offers us just three possibilities to choose from, best juxtaposed as:

1. Laura Cross was poisoned by her husband.
2. Laura Cross poisoned herself, accidentally.
3. Laura Cross poisoned herself, deliberately.

Confident that we will concur, Greene himself prefers the last of these, for reasons that become clear as one reads the remainder of his article. The more he writes, the more emotive his tone, as though there were something personal at stake. Deciding that she poisoned herself deliberately gives him access to a whole host of ready-made phrases, the like of

---

36 Greene, pp.60-1. He also makes a brief mention of the fable of the arsenic-eaters of Syria and of Mrs. Cross' servants' conviction that their mistress shared in this practice, but chooses not to explore the subject further.

37 Here, for once, the quality of the writing can't be blamed on my father, who simply transcribed it.

38 Summing up the case Greene makes a first mention of what I, uneasy about any kind of retrospective irony, would like to have known earlier—that Cross' is the signature which appears on his first wife's death certificate.

"quit this world," "cruel wrongs," "simple certainty," "to salvage her suffering" and so on, and allows Greene to humble himself with admiration for the

39 No orange pencil here either.

> single-mindedness [needed] to go ahead with such a plan [...] in order that he who had betrayed her deepest trust should be convicted, by the simple substitution of her own crime for his.

Why? With no small relish, Greene concludes: "*She was indeed, 'a woman scorned'.*"³⁹

The bulk of the file my father has given me is what I call Rozencrantz and Guildenstern material: photocopied records of other, vaguely similar cases, newspaper clippings with some nugget on one of the walk-on characters, family-trees full of empty boxes, that kind of thing. Even so, on my second night at home, though I still hadn't decided what tack to take with my speech, let alone written it—I found myself sifting through the file, to read again those pieces I'd found entertaining or curious, and which could be appreciated in and of themselves, without any knowledge of the case to which they ultimately referred. Exactly the kind of material my father, with his very particular notion of authenticity, would want incorporated into the story he's pushing me to take on. To me, the best is a newspaper article entitled "A HANGMAN'S REMINISCENCES" (subtitled "HOW BERRY DISGUISED HIMSELF IN CORK"):

> On Tuesday Berry, the executioner, after having carried out a double execution at Hereford, took the train for Birmingham and on the way confided his reminiscences to his fellow passengers in a most remarkable manner. He said—"Let me

tell you about the time I went to Cork to hang Dr. Cross; in order to elude the crowd waiting on the platform I made myself up in a pair of black eyes with charcoal. I bound my head as if my skull had been recently broken, and put some horse halters around my waist. Once outside I asked what was everyone looking after, and on hearing the name Berry, said I would not go two yards to see a creature of such a profession, and so I got quietly away to the goal [sic]. Next morning I left again disguised as an officer with complete uniform, except the sword, with this beneath my belt—"And here Berry pulled a revolver out of his pocket, frightening several of the female members of his audience. He informed us that he had taught his wife to use it as a precaution, against burglars or other attackers. Replying to a fellow traveler Berry bid us take note that his was a scientific mode of hanging, and that he did not altogether approve of the old plan of letting them struggle for a quarter of an hour. He broke their neck, and they suffered no more pain than the prick of a pin—though he added that it must be a dreadful thing for them to feel themselves going off the trap, not knowing where to, an opinion concurred with by all present. He was, he added, very particular as to what company he kept, and believed himself to be the only executioner who ever mixed with magistrates, earls, baronets, lords and dukes, and this on a regular and ongoing basis. When attending to carry out an execution he was obliged to sleep in the gaol. He had slept in 52 prisons. In his opinion it would be better to send all people condemned to death to London. They might be hanged there in batches—he could hang a dozen as easily as two.[40]

To my mind, the worst is an epic poem (so-called) by a local woman. For years I knew her only as an old drinking friend

of my father's, and that was more than enough for me—but now I'll have to start thinking of her as my father's wife. He planted the poem on the very top of the pile, as though it might act as some kind of epigraph. It was a shrewd move. I won't be able to pretend ignorance when she asks if I've come across it, as she undoubtedly will in the days to come, knowing what it is I do and probably eager to find some common ground between us. Here's an extract that's fairly representative of the whole:

> The local surgeon, going off far away
> For a full fortnight's hard-earned holiday,
> Handed over his patient-list to the charge
> Of that queer old Sasanach at large
> The more infamous than famous Dr. Cross, who was not
>   long after hanged
> For doing in his dear wife. The doctor was wronged
> Here I would swear, although he declared
> An hour before being hanged how little he did care
> For this blow of ill-wind, feeling sure
> He'd done plenty of other things he certainly deserved to
>   swing for.

Although he's lovingly transcribed a select few, my father has simply Xeroxed most of the newspaper accounts of the trial. Sometimes, on one of these foolscap sheets, amidst the masses of tightly-printed text there'll be a mere square-inch concerning the case, saying—for instance—that proceedings have been temporarily adjourned. The adjacent articles, of course, are meant to be ignored as utterly irrelevant. For example, one of those I've come across is about some dinner the Earl of Grey[41] attended at Edinburgh:

[41] Not, unfortunately, a little research of my own has shown, the one who gave his name to the tea.

The Pavilion in which his lordship was entertained was most magnificently arrayed, and palatial in proportion, such that in the course of the night's reveries one was inclined to forget that the proceedings were taking place on the terra firma of a common field. The Pavilion was supported by sixteen pillars with gilt capitals, the shafts being surrounded with wreaths of gilt laurel. The walls were ornamented with appropriate devices. After dinner, by way of introduction to he whom we had all come to hear, the Lord Advocate briefly proposed the health of the Earl of Durham (cheers) and the reformers of England. (Immense cheering.) The Earl himself came forward amidst the most rapturous cheering, which gave way to respectful silence once he commenced to speak. "How often have we been told by our Tory opponents—for you must allow me to use an expression which they are ashamed of, and have therefore dropped—how often have we been told by our Tory opponents that the spirit of reform was dying away, that liberal feelings were no longer predominant, and that the day was fast approaching, when the people of England would return like repentant sinners to their Tory homes, to be received with forgiveness by their Tory master! (Cheers and great laughter.) Can any such absurd and wanton abandonment of your hardly won and inestimable privileges be read in these proceedings of to-day? No is the answer. No; the gathering of this day—to use a Scottish phrase (cheers)—at which are the wisest, the best, and the most influential persons in Scotland, proves, without a doubt, the contrary. I have now been some twenty years in public life, during which time I have felt it both duty and pleasure to act with my noble relative, differing from him occasionally, as all men of independence must occasionally differ from one another, but following him steadily and firmly in all the great objects of his political life (cheers) and I now tell you what I believe him to be—an unflinching but safe and practical reformer—a determined corrector of all abuses, upholding the legitimate influence of the crown and the due privileges of the nobility, but at the same time advocating the extension of the liberties of the people, and their adaptation to the increased and increasing intelligence of the age. (Loud cheers.) One word more and I have done. (Cries of, 'No, no, go on.') My noble and learned relative and friend has been pleased to give me some advice, which I have no doubt he deems very sound, to some class of persons—I know nor mix with none such—who evince too strong a desire to get rid of ancient abuses. Now I frankly confess that I am one of those persons who see with regret every hour which passes over the existence of recognized and unreformed abuses. (Immense cheering.) I am, however, perfectly willing to accept the correction of them as deliberately as our good rulers, and my noble friend among them, can wish, but on one condition alone—that every measure should be proposed in conformity with those common principles for which we all contend." (Prolonged cheering.)

The newspaper report is not cut off here exactly, but about half an inch further down—in line with the end of the article my father had fixed on. Certainly, the report runs beyond this, but I've no idea of what or even how much is excluded.

DANIEL BORZUTZKY lives in Chicago, Illinois and teaches English as Second Language. His recent work has appeared in *Columbia, LVNG, The Journal of Experimental Fiction*, and *The Minus Times.*

ROBERT COOVER is the author of many novels, including *Briar Rose, The Public Burning, Gerald's Party,* and *Pinocchio in Venice.* His honors include fellowships from the Guggenheim Foundation and the National Endowment for the Arts. He teaches electronic and experimental writing at Brown University. His latest novel, *Raw Footage*, is forthcoming.

CYNTHIA CRUZ's poems have appeared or are forthcoming in *Chelsea, The New Orleans Review,* and *Pleiades.* Recent honors include fellowships at Yaddo and The MacDowell Colony. Her manuscript, *The Summon*, was a finalist for the Poetry Society of America's Alice Fay di Castagnola Award. She lives in New York City and works for Teachers and Writers.

RUTH DANON is the author of *Triangulation from a Known Point*, published by Blue Moon Books (1990). Her work has appeared in *Fence, Bomb, The Paris Review,* and *The Gettysburg Review,* among other places. She teaches at NYU where she directs the creative and expository writing program for the McGhee Division. This is her second appearance in *3rd bed.*

MARK DeCARTERET was born in Lowell, MA and has lived primarily in New Hampshire ever since. His work has appeared recently in *Conduit, The Contemporary Review, FLASH!POINT, Hunger Magazine,* and *Phoebe.* His second chapbook, *The Great Apology,* will be published this fall by Oyster River Press. He is also the author of the chapbook *Over Easy* (Minotaur, 1990) and *Review: A Book of Poems* (Kettle of Fish Press, 1995).

PATRICIA EAKINS, author of *The Hungry Girls and Other Stories* and *The Marvelous Adventures of Pierre Baptiste,* has been awarded the Aga Khan Prize, the Capricorn Prize, the NYU Press Prize for Fiction, and two NEA fellowships. Her fiction has appeared in *The Iowa Review, The Paris Review, Parnassus, Storia, Conjunctions, ALC,* and *Cahiers Charles V.* "The Hungry Girls" was adapted for theater by Collision Theory. Eakins edits *Frigate: The Transverse Review of Books* (frigatezine.com).

ELAINE EQUI is the author of many books including *Surface Tension, Decoy*, and most recently, *Voice-Over*, which won the San Francisco State Poetry Award.

MICHAEL IVES is a musician, composer, and writer. His work with the performance trio, F'loom, has been featured on National Public Radio, the CBC, and in the international anthology of sound poetry, *Homo Sonorus*. Most recently, his work appears in *New American Writing, Exquisite Corpse, Hunger*, and *Fracture*.

CAROLINE GILMAN (1794-1888) was born in Boston, but lived and worked for most of her life in Charleston, South Carolina. Her other published work includes *Recollections of a New England Bride, Recollections of a Southern Matron, Verses of a Lifetime*, and two prognostication game books similar to the one excerpted here: *Oracles from the Poets* and *The Sibyl, or, New Oracles from the Poets*.

RAY GONZALEZ is the author of *Memory Fever* (University of Arizona Press), a memoir about growing up in the Southwest, and *Turtle Pictures* (Arizona), a prose poem memoir. He is also the author of seven books of poetry, including the forthcoming *The Hawk Temple at Tierra Grande*. His first book of fiction, *The Ghost of John Wayne and Other Stories* is forthcoming from Arizona this year along with *The Underground Heart: Essays from Hidden Landscapes* in 2002.

CORMAC JAMES lives in Dublin, Ireland. His first novel, *Track and Field*, was published last year.

CHRISTOPHER KENNEDY's collection of prose poems, *Nietzsche's Horse*, was published by Mitki/Mitki Press in September, 2001. His work has appeared or will appear in *Grand Street, Ploughshares, Heliotrope, Mississippi Review*, and many other journals and magazines. He coordinates the MFA Program in Creative Writing at Syracuse University.

NORMAN LOCK has published fiction in leading journals in the US and abroad. He was awarded the Aga Khan Prize in 1979, given by *The Paris Review*. His stage plays have been performed internationally. *The House of Correction* was voted one of the 10 best plays by *The LA Times* in 1988 and (for its revival) in 1994. It was also called "the best new play of the [1996 Edinburgh Theatre] Festival." It is available from Broadway Play Publishing Company. His radio plays are broadcast by WDR, Germany. He is also the author of a work produced by The American Film Institute. The texts published here, together with a second prose sequence, are collected in a limited edition book available from elimae Books (elimae.com).

PETER MARKUS' fiction has appeared in *Black Warrior Review, New Orleans Review, Quarterly West, Third Coast*, as well as electronically in the current *failbetter.com* and a sequence of 14 fictions forthcoming in the next issue of *5_trope*.

CHAD McCAIL, born in England, lives and works in Edinburgh. Since the early Nineties, his work has appeared in many international and regional group and solo exhibitions. Public collections include the British Council Collection, the Cake Foundation (Zurich), the Cité de Genève, the Mamco (Geneva), the Scottish National Gallery of Modern Art, the City Art Centre (Edinburgh), and the Musée d'Art Moderne Grand Duc Jean (Luxemburg).

BRYSON NEWHART's writing is forthcoming in *Both Magazine* and can be found in *The American Journal of Print, Insurance Magazine, Pindeldyboz*, and on the websites *elimae, Casajp, Pindeldyboz, Dairyaire, The Minus Times*, and the *McSweeney's* letters pages.

MARK O'NEIL is a freelance writer living and working in Saratoga Springs, New York. His work has appeared in *5_trope* and *The Cortland Review*.

KIM PARKO lives in Santa Fe with her mentor/doodledog Kholi. She writes, makes art, and will be teaching art at a local public elementary school. Lately she's been tending to her tiny garnden in the hopes that it will flourish in the midst of inhospitable soil.

KATHRYN RANTALA has work in the recent *American Journal of Print, elimae, Pig Iron Malt,*

Café Irreal, and is upcoming in *Spinning Jenny*, *Tatlin's Tower* and others. She is the founder and coeditor of *Snow Monkey, an Eclectic Journal*.

Two of RAPPEL's novels, *Mabel in her Twenties* and *transiT* (both by Rosaire Appel) have been published by FC2, and excerpts from a third work *Radiooil* have appeared in *Fiction International*. Besides writing, she makes and exhibits photographs and digital drawings.

KEVIN SAMPSELL lives and works in Portland, Oregon. His writing has appeared in *The Stranger*, *2 girls review*, *Plazm*, *Web Del Sol*, *5_trope*, and *McSweeney's*. He has authored many small books that can be very hard to find.

ROBYN SCHIFF's poems have appeared or are forthcoming in *Black Warrior Review*, *Explosive*, *Fence*, *Volt*, and *Verse*. She lives in Brooklyn with her husband.

ALAN SONDHEIM's books include the anthology *Being on Line: Net Subjectivity* (Lusitania, 1996), *Disorders of the Real* (Station Hill, 1988), and *echo* (alt-X digital arts, 2001) as well as numerous other chapbooks, books, and articles. Sondheim co-moderates several email lists, including *Cybermind*, *Cyberculture*, and *Wryting*.

VIRGIL SUÁREZ was born in Havana, Cuba. He is the author of four novels, *The Cutter*, *Latin Jazz*, *Havana Thursdays*, and *Going Under*, and of a collection of stories, *Welcome to the Oasis*. His memoirs, *Spared Angola: Memories of a Cuban-American Childhood* and *Cafe Nostalgia: Writings from the Hyphen*, chronicle his life of exile in both Cuba and the United States. He is the author of three collections of poetry: *Garabato Poems*, *You Come Singing*, and *In the Republic of Longing*. He has two new books forthcoming: *Palm Crows* (University of Arizona Press) and *Banyan* (LSU Press).

MANDEE WRIGHT is from Colorado and types for a living. She regularly consoles crying people over the telephone.

"Oracles of Youth" is excerpted from *Oracles for Youth* by Caroline Gilman. New York: Putnam & Co., 1852.

Chad McCail's *Alien Genital* appears courtesy of Laurent Delaye Gallery, London, Collection the Musée d'Art Moderne Grand Duc Jean, Luxemburg. The cover art is a detail from this series.

Norman Lock's "Opera with Moon Snails" first appeared electronically in *5_trope*.

Chris Kennedy's "Decomposition #249," "Trivia," & "The Broken Lock" appear in *Nietzsche's Horse*, Nitki/Nitki Press, 2001.

Patricia Eakins' "The Other Side" appears in *Reading Eakins*, ed. Francoise Palleau. France: University of Orleans, 2001.

"Lucky Pierre Thaws Out" Copyright © 2001 by Robert Coover.